The Divided Heart of Catherine Mackerras

THE
DIVIDED HEART
OF CATHERINE MACKERRAS

Faith, family & self-understanding in a different Australia

PATRICK MULLINS

Copyright © 2024 Patrick Mullins

ALL RIGHTS RESERVED. This book contains material protected under International and Federal Copyright Laws and Treaties. Any unauthorised reprint or use of this material is prohibited. No part of this book may be reproduced or transmitted in any form or by any means, electronic or mechanical, including photocopying, recording, or by any information storage and retrieval system without express written permission from the publisher.

Published by Connor Court Publishing under the imprint The Kapunda Press. The Kapunda Press is an imprint of Connor Court Publishing in association with the PM Glynn Institute, Australian Catholic University.

CONNOR COURT PUBLISHING PTY LTD

PO Box 7257
Redland Bay QLD 4165
sales@connorcourt.com www.connorcourt.com

Cover picture: Cover picture: Elric Ringstad, Untitled 3 (c. 2019), oil, bees wax, damar on canvas

ISBN: (pbk.) 9781923224247

Cover design by Ian James

Printed in Australia

"To relate past actions is comparatively easy, given honesty and a retentive memory. To relate past thoughts and feelings is a delicate and exacting task."

Catherine Mackerras

Contents

Foreword		xi
I.	A different country	1
II.	The cool depths of a great church	5
III.	Milosz's dictum	33
IV.	Perfect wives and perfect mothers	59
Acknowledgements		73
Notes		75

Foreword

Dallas McInerney

The aim and mission of Catholic Schools NSW is to help in bringing to life the Catholic Church's evangelising mission. I am inspired by the work that all our Catholic school principals and teachers do for our students in this regard. Every journey of conversion is unique, and so it is important that we support everyone who goes on their own journey. The story of Catherine Mackerras's conversion to the Catholic Church is perhaps no more unique than any other, however, it throws light on many aspects of Australian religious and social history that are rarely seen today.

Catherine Mackerras's memoirs, *Divided Heart*, provide a remarkable picture of Australian society in the first half of the twentieth century. She vividly paints a picture of a sectarian and class-conscious Sydney that few of us ever knew. She also articulates the way in which the Catholic intellectual tradition spoke to her heart as well as to her mind. Hers is a fascinating story of how acting in Truth and Love can speak to an unbeliever. It is a reminder of the special role of Catholic schools and universities in fostering this wonderful tradition.

More than half a century has passed since *Divided Heart* was written and life in Sydney and Australia at large has changed profoundly since then. Dr Patrick Mullins has used his visiting fellowship at the PM Glynn Institute to write an essay reflecting on *Divided Heart*. His award-winning 2020 biography, *Tiberius with a Telephone: the life and stories of Willaim McMahon*, was an important study of political leadership at the national level. Thus, it is surprising to discover the unexpected doors that he opens in this book, and to find him writing about quite different matters. Bringing his formidable skills as a biographer to *Divided Heart*, he examines the way in which the author understands her own conversion story; ponders the strange lacunas in her narrative; and reflects on some of the more profound ways in which aspects of the Australia of Catherine Mackerras have changed in the last half-century.

As such, there is much for us to glean about Australia, the Catholic Church, and evangelisation from *The Divided Heart of Catherine Mackerras*. For all these reasons, Catholic Schools NSW has been pleased to have the opportunity to support the PM Glynn Institute at Australian Catholic University, in publishing Dr Mullins's essay.

The PM Glynn Institute provides ACU with a vital link between the University, the Church, and the wider community. ACU is first and foremost a Catholic university. As such, it is committed to the pursuit of knowledge, the dignity of the human person, and the common good within the Catholic intellectual tradition. This demands contributing not only to the religious life of the Church, but to the broader cultural life of the Church, and its place in

Australian society. I'm always excited by the thought that ACU can enable innovative contributions to the Catholic intellectual tradition in Australia, and thoughtful reflections on the pursuit of Truth in Love that so captured the heart of Catherine Mackerras.

I am grateful to Dr Michael Casey, director of the PM Glynn Institute, for commissioning this volume, and to Dr Mullins for bringing Mrs Mackerras's *Divided Heart* to life for our generation.

Dallas McInerney
CEO, Catholic Schools NSW

I
A different country

Sectarianism has proved to be an oddly resilient strain in Australian life. Like the shingles, it seems to appear from nowhere, inflict considerable pain, and then go quiet again, as though biding its time. It first appeared in the 1840s amid high Irish immigration and the first colonial elections; then it vanished amid the gold rushes. It came back again in the mid-1860s; faded; and then returned, virulently, during the upheaval of First World War, the conscription debates, and the 1916 Easter Rising. But this bout of sectarianism, though it left significant and enduring legacies, also spurred a renewed resistance to any return. Unless one counts controversy over the handling of child sexual abuse by religious institutions — and some do — sectarianism appears to have vanished from modern Australian life.

When I have spoken with people who lived through its tail-end, in the 1960s and 1970s, their recollections of sectarianism are always delivered in a tone of bemusement — as though it is not quite believable that this prejudice, this product of strong religious motivation, could ever have shaped the makeup of government departments, made for unspoken 'bars' to employment in certain places, divided children through their attendance at different schools, and ruled off who married whom. It seems wholly at odds in Australia — this secular, supposedly laid-back country. Doesn't it?

This is one reason to value Catherine Mackerras's memoirs, *Divided Heart*. An account of her journey from Protestantism to Catholicism at the heights of that most recent period of sectarianism, the book is evidence of the enormous gulf that once separated Australians. Though *Divided Heart* is not overly concerned with the prejudices that sectarianism aroused, it is in many ways a picture of how religion shapes a society, cultivating different attitudes that interlink with institutions and individuals.

Divided Heart is also a reminder of the profound changes that Australia has undergone in the last century. At the time of Catherine's birth, in 1900, more than 90 per cent of the country claimed to be Christian. Thirty years later, at the time of her conversion, this had fallen to 85 per cent, with Anglicanism (38 per cent) and Catholicism (19 per cent) the most nominated faiths. Thirty years later again, at the time Catherine wrote *Divided Heart*, the proportion of Christians was still strong but the demographics were changing: 34.9 per cent for Anglicanism, 24.9 per cent for Catholicism. Another thirty years later, when *Divided Heart* was published, Anglicanism had dropped to 23.8 per cent and Catholicism had reached a near high watermark, of 27.3 per cent. Christianity was still the most common religion in Australia, but the decline from there was precipitous. By 2021, the proportion of Australians professing to be Christian had halved (43.9 per cent) and those claiming to be Anglican or Catholic had plummeted, Anglicans most of all. Simultaneously, the proportion claiming no religious affiliation has grown from almost nothing at the time of

Catherine's birth to almost a third of the country in 2021.¹ (There is an even sharper change in the way that 'no religious affiliation' has been understood: in Catherine's childhood, atheism and agnosticism were synonymous with 'rationalism', and the 1911 census famously stated that people could respond that they had no religion if they were a 'free thinker, or if no denomination or religion'. Today, the 'no religious affiliation' category includes an enormous number of spiritual and secular beliefs — from humanism to unitarian universalism — *as well as* atheism and agnosticism).

The transformation might make it difficult to understand, in the mid-2020s, Catherine's conversion to Catholicism and the barriers she had to contend with. The dominant Christianity and rife sectarianism that were facts of life for her can seem, to a reader in a determinedly secular Australia, just too different to be imagined. The theology and doctrines she wrestles with are also strikingly different to contemporary accounts of religiosity, which tend to stress the spiritual dimensions of religion, the quest for individual meaning, and eschew any discussion of institutions in that religion. Reading *Divided Heart* underscores L.P. Hartley's famous line: 'The past is a different country.'

And yet reading *Divided Heart*, and grappling with what Catherine writes, is rewarding. *Divided Heart* has much to say about issues that many people still face. There is a thorough and lively exploration of the influences that may act on a person — family, culture, geography, art, religion, personality — as they are formed and grow up. There is a telling account of the importance of education and thinking for oneself. There are reflections, some more controversial than others, on issues that still crowd public debate — on imperialism, on gender relations, and more. Even Sydney property prices figure.

But *Dividing Heart* also leaves much that is valuable unsaid. Considering Catherine's religious journey beyond the date of her conversion — that is, considering the book against her biography — reveals much that is also relevant to a contemporary readership. There is the tension between personal authenticity and communal belonging. There are the roles that we perform with different audiences and people. There are the rifts that may suddenly appear in relationships hitherto solid. There is the reckoning with identity and how we might see ourselves.

And, above all, there are the gaps and silences. It is a rote observation that no memoir, no matter how extended or confessional the author, tells everything. Even Karl Ove Knausgaard's six-volume autobiography, which delights in the most banal detail of tea-making and home-cleaning, contains evasions and gaps. But the apparent candour with which Catherine relates her early life, and the verve of her storytelling in *Divided Heart*, is such that a reader might sweep through the book without noticing the elisions in her account. In fact, it was only as this reader turned the last pages of the book — Catherine recalling the bells of St Mary's, the restless enquiries of her young mind, the cravings of her unsated heart — that these became apparent.

To understand these gaps, however, one must understand first how Catherine divided herself.

II
The cool depths of a great church

Catherine Mackerras (née Maclaurin) drafted her memoirs in 1960–61. Originally titled *Hitherto*, excerpts and fragments were published in *Twentieth Century* and the *Catholic Weekly* in 1963, possibly to test reaction ahead of full publication.[2] But she appears to have made no move to put them in book form afterward. Amid a stream of articles for various periodicals, she instead wrote a short-ish biography of her great-great-grandfather and began work on a life of her grandfather. In the wake of her husband's death, in 1973, however, she seemed to lose interest in that project, and it stalled.

Her death followed in 1977, but a kind of second life was found in 1991, when Little Hills Press published the memoirs, now titled *Divided Heart*. The book came with a foreword by son Alastair commenting on the circumstances of its composition, speculating about the reasons it was not published, and ending with a reflection on the likely uncongeniality of the modern world for Catherine Mackerras.

His sense of a woman out of her time is apt both for the character of that woman and the immense changes that took place in Australia in the twentieth century. Born at the turn of that century 'in a small mid-Victorian terrace, in a pleasant street known as Roslyn Gardens', Catherine plants her theme early. The world of her birth is prosperous and secure, she writes, but is then suddenly and ominously otherwise. The outbreak of the Boer War, in 1899, portends the decline of the British Empire, just as Catherine's burgeoning intelligence portends the end of the prejudices she absorbs as a child. Then there is the house to which the infant Catherine moves on Bayswater Road, a spacious old colonial dubbed *Tintern*. It has a wide veranda, pleasant gardens, and stables in which Flossie — the chestnut mare that pulled her father's sulky — stood stamping while being brushed to a sheen by an Irishman named Kennedy.

Tintern was demolished while Catherine was writing, and its ruin plays in the background of *Divided Heart*. At a literal level, its demolition was of a piece with what Catherine saw as the ongoing obliteration — the death, even — of the city of her childhood. According to her, Sydney circa 1900 was a 'pleasant British colonial city', with a population of half a million, languidly spread across bucolic hills and basking in a perfect golden glow. There were old cable cars running up the streets, the hillsides were spread with wildflowers and perfect for picnics, native birds sang in tall trees, and the beaches were a quiet escape from a city where motor cars were still rarities.

But nostalgia, as Freud said, is always in some way unreal, and Catherine's recollections of Sydney at the time of her birth are very partial. Only a stone's throw from that Bayswater Road home was a very different Sydney — where a motor car was an undreamt luxury, where the leisure to sit on beflowered hillsides all too scarce, where poverty and graft were in awful abundance.

Catherine's memoirs suggest she was not altogether unconscious of this different city. With a very modern Australian sensibility, Catherine gestures toward it by noting the increased cost of real estate around Bayswater Road. The cottages she saw springing up along the shore might well be 'hideous', as she thought, but the demand for space in the eastern suburbs was so palpable in the 1900s that her parents felt compelled to eschew the Edenic touches of *Tintern* when they built a new house next door. In *Strathyre*, to which the family moved when Catherine was four years old, there were no stables, no Flossie, no gardens. A square of asphalt in the back was their only concession to open spaces. Otherwise: 'The land in Bayswater Road was becoming too valuable.'

The move, and the insight, lead to Catherine's awareness of Sydney's religious landscape. From the balcony of *Strathyre*, she could spy the white yachts flecking the blue water of Rushcutters Bay; to the east, she could see the grey stone spire of St Mark's Church of England, on Darling Point. Glimpses of that habitue of the elite and moneyed provoked her curiosity: *What was going on in it?*[3]

That interest was underlined by the apparent absence of religion in the family home. Catherine's father, Charles (1872–1925), a doctor and writer, deplored religion; her mother, Anne (née Croal) (1869–1937) was a Scottish Presbyterian whose childhood had been spent doing scripture readings and playing religious games yet who, in marriage, had subordinated her faith to her spouse's rationalism. They did not go to church, did not talk of prayer, gave even no explanation of what religion was. When Catherine asked what God was, her mother tucked her in, kissed her, and uttered the line to which all parents resort when words fail: 'You'll understand more about that when you're older.' Asked the same question, her father sought the refuge of silence, then diplomacy: 'Mother would be angry if I told you what I thought.' Then, reaching for another oft-used solution for parents facing a knotty question, he told Catherine to ask her mother.[4]

This silence was plainly unsustainable. Religion was all around Catherine. The spire of St Mark's was but one example. At kindergarten, she was perplexed to see her friends fold their hands and lower their heads and murmur indecipherably; sleeping at a friend's home, later, she observed the same ritual, though this time she gleaned some mention of an 'invisible father'. 'That's the Lord's Prayer,' a friend explained.

'And who is the Lord?' Catherine asked.

'Dunno,' said the friend. 'God, I expect.'[5]

Catherine found more enlightenment from the servants working in her home — people who came from a different Sydney to that which Catherine had been born and would so fondly recall. Nurse Ella Turkington conscientiously observed the house injunction on religious teaching, but her evangelical Anglican faith nonetheless pervaded everything that she did. She sang hymns while working in the nursery and recited the Ten Commandments while helping Catherine complete multiplication tables. For this she was sent away when Catherine was seven years old. The governess who replaced her, however, was in the eyes of Catherine's father little better. This new duenna made no bones about her faith nor her disagreement with the approach adopted by Catherine's father. A few months after starting work, she took Catherine to a small, weatherboard chapel at Milsons Point. 'The congregation did not just sit still and do nothing,' Catherine writes, 'but some of them jumped up and told wonderful stories about how they had been converted.' Songs, scripture, a profound service: Catherine came home hopeful that a hymn she heard and learned was so beautiful that it might woo her father. But he proved impervious to the music (or, at least, his daughter's rendition). 'Can't you stop singing that frightful hymn?' he grizzled. 'Where did you ever hear such stuff?'

Catherine's honesty saw her governess summarily dismissed, but some kind of reckoning was near. For some time now, her parents had periodically dispatched her to the Macquarie Street home of her paternal grandparents. Now the very snarling heart of Sydney's business district, Macquarie Street then was something very different again: quieter, more modest, more residential. The old house, number 155, had gardens and disused stables and was a vantage point for immense vistas:

> Opposite it were the Botanical Gardens, stretching to the Harbour's edge, and beyond was Farm Cove, where the men-of-war were. It looked down to the great lighthouse which crowns South Head at the entrance to Port Jackson. From the top floor of the dignified early Victorian three-storey house one could see beyond the heads to the Pacific Ocean and watch the ships steaming away to England and America… It filled my soul with a romantic pleasure.

That pleasure, however, was tempered by the melancholic figure of Catherine's grandmother, an aged figure who had memories of watching corrobborees held by the Eora people in the Botanic Gardens. Her disdain for the colour of social life was compounded by her increasing deafness; already somewhat distant from her husband and even her sons, she seemed in want of nothing so much as affection — yet she seemed also to be forever denied it. Even Catherine was unwilling to provide it: 'I would struggle out of her unwelcome hugs, pushing her roughly from me.' The young Catherine saw her grandmother in pitiable terms: confined by a stroke to a wheelchair, parked by the window so that she might observe but not participate in street-life outside, increasingly speechless and, notably, religiously bereft.

When she died, Catherine's parents decided to move from *Strathyre* and live with Catherine's widowed grandfather, Sir Normand Maclaurin. A physician, an administrator, a company director, a university vice-chancellor, and a former politician, Maclaurin was in person an austere and rigid Scot with an authoritative, even imperious, manner. Catherine's father instigated the move to Macquarie Street to please his own father; back in his childhood home he 'felt himself a child' again and became unwilling to assert his prerogative as a parent (one can only imagine the reaction of Catherine's mother when told that she would now 'keep house' for her father-in-law).

With such dynamics at play it was unsurprising that Maclaurin held sway. Raised in the Presbyterian church, he still attended church each Sunday. When Catherine announced from curiosity her desire to join him, it seems her father did not feel he could deny her. It became something of a ritual thereafter: Catherine's father would play Beethoven on the family piano, and Maclaurin and Catherine would set off to the grand neo-Romantic edifice of St Stephen's, just down the street.[6] Maclaurin would usher his granddaughter into a private pew and, during the collection, deposit into the plate a sovereign; in what the young Catherine thought the highlight of the whole service, he would give her a shilling to do the same.

For the child Catherine, these weekly encounters with religion were enmeshed with the British Empire. Imperialism was a faith not quite synonymous, yet not wholly distinct, from the religious expressions she heard and observed at St Stephen's. It was a faith she wondered if her father might have been more comfortable with. Born with a view of the warships anchored in Farm Cove, Sydney Harbour, she writes, he would rise to the drum of the Royal Salute and go to sleep as the Last Post rolled across the water. When he heard Moses' Song of Deliverance in church one day — 'The Lord is a man of war: the Lord is his name,' — he believed it a reference to those ships. As Catherine notes, wryly, 'He privately equated God with the British navy.'[7]

She resisted a similar equation for the stirrings that began to preoccupy her. Time and change were the chief philosophical obstacles. News of her grandmother's death had made her aware of time's ridges, valleys, and chasms. At first, Catherine felt remorse for her youthful disdain and dismissal of her grandmother; then, in the silence that followed, she felt something else entirely. She was sitting in the swaying shade of casuarinas, with an aunt, near the beach, when she heard the news. As she described:

> I could hear the roaring of the waves of the Pacific Ocean breaking on Cronulla Beach, close by, rising and falling, joyless and

unceasing, in mighty, unrelenting rhythm. They were there all the time, of course, and usually I did not even hear them, but at that moment the breakers seemed suddenly to obtrude themselves on my consciousness as I mused on my poor grandmother. The thought came then to my mind for the first time in my life: 'We must all die! And when we are dead, the breakers will be rolling still forever and forever and forever!'

The disparity between those unceasing waves and the just-ceased life of her grandmother filled her with horror. Catherine felt suddenly insecure, doomed, weighed down by the knowledge that she and all those she loved would die. Sorting through old photographs of her grandmother a few days later, seeing in them what would inevitably be lost — youth, beauty, memory — Catherine thought of pleading with her own mother never to change, never to grow old, and above all never to die. But, simultaneous to that thought, came the knowledge that it was a promise her mother would never be able to keep.[8]

Thus, as her classmates sang *The Empire Song*, Catherine came to feel too uneasy to mouth its proclamations of eternity: 'Other empires have existed, and have crumbled to decay, but this Union close cemented shall never pass away.' Her awareness that everyone dies and all things eventually pass made it impossible for her to regard the British Empire as an eternal force, let alone synonymous with religion. Amid the singing of her classmates, she quietly rephrased the last line in a way that gestured to her anguished knowledge of death and her ambivalence about the offering of a false god, in the British Empire: '*May* it never pass away.'[9]

Catherine's grandfather would not exactly assuage that anguish about eternity. Once, snorting at an overly sentimental biography of Marie Antoinette that Catherine had won at school, Maclaurin retrieved his copy of Thomas Carlyle's *French Revolution*. 'Time is done,' he read, apparently oblivious to her falling face, 'all the scaffolding of Time falls wretched with hideous clangour round thy soul…' Moreover, despite taking his granddaughter to church, he was also antipathetic toward religion. Books had done their work on him: 'The teachings of Calvinism he had learnt at his mother's knee had faded before the onslaught of eighteenth and nineteenth century rationalism and agnosticism. Hume and Gibbon, Darwin and Huxley, John Stuart Mill and especially Herbert Spencer, had undermined the authority of Presbyterian orthodoxy.'[10]

And yet religion and religious difference remained palpable in this gloomy home, and again it was the people from a different Sydney that most made it so. With Maclaurin ensconced in his study, with Catherine's father occupying the dining room with patients, and with her mother seemingly invisible, the child's curiosity was excited downstairs: by the cook sweating over a mammoth fuel stove in an airless basement, by the parlourmaids who used a little lift to move food from the kitchen to the dining room, by the butler who would remove his coat to shine cutlery. All were Catholic, employed by Maclaurin because he believed them to be more honest and harder working than other servants.

The sectarianism from which this prejudice emanated was a palpable feature of Australian society at the time of Catherine's childhood. Anti-Catholic prejudice was among the first European imports to Australia, present in the disdain nursed by British gaolers toward their Irish wards and coalescing around class discriminations as the colonies took root. Political movements and rebellions in the home countries reinforced the prejudice, which was further entrenched by events including Cardinal Patrick Moran's candidacy for the federation conventions in the 1890s (which led to cries of 'Protestants, beware! There is something dearer than federation!') and the rapid emergence of the Labor Party in the 1890s.

In the circles among which Catherine's family moved, Catholics were subjects of scorn and disapproval. Catholic antipathy for the British Empire made them 'reprobates', Catherine recalled — worse even than the Boers. Catherine's childhood ambivalence for the British Empire made her a smidge less hostile to Catholics, but she was simultaneously intrigued by their faith and repelled by the gaudy, sometimes gauche tokens of it: the medals, the altars, the holy pictures, the cloying incense. 'They affected me with a mixture of repulsion and attraction.'[11]

The attraction informed Catherine's love of hearing the bells of St Mary's Cathedral each morning; it spurred her to watch from her bed as the housemaids walked to mass; it even prompted her to alight early from a tram to enter the Cathedral while enroute to school. 'I pushed open the heavy leather door and shyly walked in, out of the bright Australian sunshine, to the cool depths of the great church.' But the repulsion was just as visceral as the attraction and it kicked within moments: 'There were a number of people kneeling in front of the white marble altar, but before I had time to see any more, panic seized me, and I fled as fast as I could.'[12]

The panic was in one sense the result of her awareness that

she had crossed a line. Her father's antipathy for religion, her mother's suppressed Presbyterianism, her grandfather's dual (and duelling) rationalist and Calvinist sympathies, and the prejudice of Catherine's social class, meant that any kind of interest in Catholicism was, fundamentally, rebellion. 'The Roman Catholic Church stood high in the list of things to be avoided,' she wrote, 'along with the Labor Party, with which it was apparently allied.'

And yet a line had been crossed. 'I had *seen* the Catholic Church; I had realised its presence.' And from that moment, she reflected later, there was no going back.[13]

*

In *Divided Heart*, Catherine acknowledged that it was impossible to know the clarity with which she understood all this, let alone the depth to which she understood it, as a child:

> How hard it is to trace, after the space of forty years, the interaction of thought and sentiment, the alternate shrinking back and springing forward, the changing moods, the anxious questionings, the distrust of one's own mental processes, and particularly of instinctive and subconscious processes, the periods when thought of any kind seems hopeless, when feeling is numb, when reason and emotion have alike failed us! To relate past actions is comparatively easy, given honesty and a retentive memory. To relate past thoughts and feelings is a delicate and exacting task.[14]

She was aware, too, of the chief imperative of a memoir — to match the person on the page with the person writing the book — and the distortion that complete subservience to this imperative creates. Some memoirists, looking back on the spectral figure that they once were, think about the person they could have been instead and what they might have done. In *Real Estate*, the third volume of her 'living autobiography', British writer Deborah Levy speculates about the kind of person she imagined she could have been, and still might be in the second life afforded by literature:

> If I could not find her in real life, why not invent her on the page? There she is, steering her high horse with flair, making sure she does not run over girls and women struggling to find a horse of their own. Does she scoop them up and ride the high horse with them? Do they scoop her up and take over the reins? Did that feel true? I hoped so. My fifties had been a time of change and turbulence, energetic and exciting. A time of self-respect and perhaps a sort of homecoming. So, there you are! Where have you been all these years?[15]

The artefacts of those years, however, may also prove to be an anchor. In the same volume, Levy writes of finding a two decade-old Christmas card inscribed by her then-husband promising a thousand years of devotion. The elision of time and the lapse of that devotion leaves Levy simultaneously drawn to but also repelled from the woman who received that card. She tries to remember that woman, herself, but not too clearly: the thought that her younger self might be aghast at her future self, and the thought in turn that Levy might apprehend her younger self with disappointment, makes for contact that is shy and shying. 'She and I,' writes Levy, eventually, 'haunted each other across time.'[16]

There is a slight sense of haunting in *Divided Heart*. Catherine spies her youthful foolishness, her prejudices, and her angst. She owns up to instances of her limited comprehension as a child. She does it, artfully, in a way that does not conceal the reality from her readers. Estrangement is her chief technique: the description offered of her schoolfriends' night-time prayers (they 'murmured under their breath') has just enough in it to explain Catherine's bafflement, give the clue to what those friends are doing, and to make the reader think about the strangeness of observed prayer. On other occasions, she offered a striking depiction of the ways in which adults respond to that estrangement when children articulate it. Catherine saw a sign in a park declaring that trespassers on the grass would be prosecuted. She asked an adult whether it was a prayer — trespassers having 'a familiar sound' from the prayers of those schoolfriends. The adult burst out laughing: 'What an idea!'

But the child created on the page is also coloured by Catherine's strong, adult personality. The harsh words on her grandmother — 'Really rather a stupid woman and unworthy of the distinguished man she had married' — are not those of a child. Nor is the detection of the dynamics between her grandfather and father. The picture she offers of a golden, turn-of-the-century Sydney reads as especially burnished, too — as though her pen was hurried by her revulsion with her home city at the time of her writing. Catherine's disdain for 'progress' in its most banal invocations infects her prose and prevents her from seeing any redeeming feature in that progress. 'The relentless bulldozer has uprooted many a tall tree where native birds abounded,' she writes, early on. 'Rows of hideous cottages line the shores of still creeks by whose banks we lazed while the billy boiled. Suburbia has spread her tentacles far and wide.'[17] Alienation from the city and a preference for the bucolic is something of a cliché, but the unequivocal preference and the willingness to insist upon it is consistent with the personality that animates the pages of *Divided Heart*.

As Alastair Mackerras notes in his foreword, Catherine had a 'very strong personality': she dominated her household and 'presided over' dinner table conversation. In many ways, it is hard to see how such a personality could write about the uncertainty of religious faith and the journey required to resolve that uncertainty by finding some kind of truth. In a lengthy passage that cast all she had related before this as 'childish things', Catherine avers whether that uncertainty was (or is) even real:

> We have travelled on our own account towards the city, yet we have been impelled thereto by grace. We have pressed onward to our goal as though alone, yet an irresistible guide has been beside us. How can we understand this paradox, this seeming reconciliation of irreconcilables? The interaction of grace and free will has been from time immemorial among the greatest of the mysteries. Who am I that I should solve it?[18]

And yet her very endeavour with the pen is aimed at solving it. As a literary genre, writes the American literary scholar Patrick Riley, autobiography has long been preoccupied with religious conversion. 'From Augustine and Abelard to Bunyan and Guyon, to Rousseau and Renan, to Sartre and Malcolm X, the experience and the language of subjective metamorphosis are woven like a golden thread through the most disparate examples of the autobiographical genre.'[19] While the form of that conversion has, especially in more contemporary works of autobiography, become increasingly secular in nature, it remains true that the metamorphosis is the structuring element, the rough trajectory that writers traces as they try to understand their experiences. Philippe Lejeune, the authoritative and perceptive surveyor of autobiography as a literary genre and philosophical exercise, has argued that conversion gives order to that experience by creating a reference point from which the writer might understand how they have constructed their identity out of the chaos of their life.[20] Conversion also allows the writer, in a more therapeutic sense, to resolve through embodiment the contradictions of that chaos by creating a unified, rather than divided, self.

Notwithstanding that she curates the material included, the chaos and divisions that Catherine traces in *Divided Heart* are notable. It is not merely that, as a child, she was surrounded by adults of differing religious faiths and outlooks; it was that, as a child, she was pulled between those faiths and outlooks. And just as it became unsustainable for her to be kept ignorant of what others understood God to be, it was unsustainable that she should be pulled from the rationalism of her father to the Presbyterianism of her mother and grandfather, from the Protestant faiths of her social class to the jingoistic faith in the British Empire that blanketed her country. It was unsustainable that she should remain curious and yet revolted by the Catholic Church; it was unsustainable that everything should decay and die and yet somehow there exists an eternal. Resolving these tensions was, in this sense, inevitable.

These tensions and the need for their resolution, which are at the core of *Divided Heart*, do co-exist with another. Woven around the discussion of her family, of religion, and of Empire, are women of profoundly different ilk and temperament, each existing in different bounds of freedom and restriction. There is tension in what they suggest is possible for women — and for Catherine. The way in which Catherine's mother has compromised on her faith, in marriage, is contrasted by the religiosity of Catherine's nurse and governess. The prejudices and ossified ways of her dour Presbyterian maternal aunts Priscilla, Caroline, and Frances — flinty, tragic figures, in many respects — are thrown into sharp relief by the partial freedom won by her aunt Sally, who not-so-secretly converted to Anglo-Catholicism while away from home. When she comes to stay with Catherine's family in Australia, Sally drapes an ostentatiously large, wooden rosary next to her bed and plasters the walls of her room with religious prints. But when Catherine dares to pick up a silver crucifix Sally snatches it back — as though afraid that her hosts might object.

Far away from Catherine's parents, on a trip through France, Sally is more relaxed — 'light-hearted as a bird,' Catherine writes — and publicly religious. She ushers Catherine into a Catholic church, in Marseilles, saying that they must give thanks for their safe voyage and light a candle in prayer. When Catherine, from astounded shame, says Sally should not be 'so Roman Catholic', her aunt simply grins: 'The attitude of your parents to the Roman Catholic Church is a very foolish one!'[21] As if to drum that in (and, perhaps, to alleviate the dependence instilled by being a guest in Catherine's home) she then leads her niece in and out of a series of Catholic churches, lighting further candles and talking about the statues, ornaments, and other Gothic splendours in 'paroxysms of effusive admiration'.[22]

But by the time Catherine sees Sally again, however, a few years later, a change is underway. Catherine perceives Sally's Anglo-Catholicism to be on the back foot, under siege from an intellectual agnosticism that is fostered by Sally's feminist friends, including a philandering professor who almost induces Sally to elope with him.[23] Catherine is sceptical about the agnosticism, even as she notes her father's delight in it, and she deplores the feminist desire for independence that leads those friends to look down on Catherine's mother. She is rocked, too, by the letters Sally sends urging her not to be a 'parasite' on her father.

Another collision is in the offing. Catherine prizes the education she received from Margaret Hodge and Harriet Newcomb, two Englishwomen who came to Sydney and opened a kindergarten, Shirley, in 1900. Newcomb was a specialist in children's education and fundamentally conventional; Hodge was an historian, a suffragist, and an eccentric but perfect 'blue stocking'. Catherine found them uniquely able to arouse and hold their students' attention, and she delighted in the encouragement they offered to perceive connections across a diverse syllabus. Her years under their tutelage, Catherine said, were the happiest of her childhood and the departure of both women from Australia were dark clouds: 'The educational sun did indeed cease to shine for me for many a long day afterwards.'[24]

No sun was in evidence at St Felix's, the Anglican girls' boarding school that Catherine began attending in Derbyshire in 1915–16. It was an unhappy interlude for Catherine, who missed her family and the Australian sun. The typically adolescent experience was, in *Divided Heart*, given a retrospective gloss via the disquiet Catherine projects from the vantage point of the 1960s. In her view, classes at St Felix's were directed at training girls much as boys were trained and with a similar objective — professional excellence. This was a break from Western European tradition and created marital tension by introducing competition between men and women. As Catherine writes:

> The Christian ideal of woman as the helpmate of man can only be carried into practice with great difficulty in the face of the modern economic independence and intellectual training of women... The typical twentieth century attitude of women to life which is fostered by the education of girls in the belief in their economic independence of men, in their intellectual equality to men, and complete social freedom in their relations to men, sets up a formidable barrier against completely Christian living, and undoubtedly complicates matrimonial problems to a great degree.[25]

Read in twenty-first century Australia, the passage certainly prompts a raised eyebrow. One reason is Catherine's untroubled agreement with that apparently 'Christian ideal' of woman only as a helpmate of man: it does not entirely sound like her to be so uncritical. Another is the lack of any scrutiny of the role of men in this: should their education or role change? Yet another reason to look askance is the implication that the economic and social changes of the last sixty years must have resulted in a colossal failure of 'completely Christian living'. Is that reasonable?

Yet another reason for this passage to be so striking is the autobiographical reading that it suggests. No one would accuse Catherine of lacking educational training; she also had some financial means of her own during married life. Is she blaming these, then, for the problems that did arise in her marriage?

Writing in 1960–61, Catherine may well not have been conscious that this reading was possible. Instead, she put forward the experience at St Felix as another spur to turn away from the Protestant churches of her family, social class, and environment. Thus, her dismissal of Church of England schools as vessels for promulgating narrow English ideas about class, and her admiration for Catholic schools, whose wide, holistic view meant that they alone could combine modern intellectual ideals with the 'chief work' of women, the work 'for which she was created'. And what was that? According the Catherine, it was simple: 'Her function as wife and mother'.[26]

*

For all the tensions created in the first half of *Divided Heart*, its trajectory in the second half is clear and the resolution is inevitable. Following that early brief visit to St Mary's Cathedral, in Sydney, Catherine encounters the Catholic Church again and again. On each occasion, her instinctive aversion fades a little more; she becomes chary of the social stigma of Catholicism; she notes with regret the way she and friends treated a French teacher who confessed to voting, as a Catholic in the 1920s would be expected, for the Labor Party.

Catholicism also gives her relief from the 'mournful sense of fleeting time' that oppressed her so heavily when her grandmother died. The early horror of discovering that Aunt Sally is an 'idolater' is unsettled by the strange experience of encountering 'the atmosphere of faith' in the French churches Sally leads her through. The feeling arising in those solemn, 'mysterious silences' is new, palpable, and provocative. Catherine refuses to write or conceive of it in the same breath as prayer but wonders whether numinousness — as she lightly suggests — encapsulates it. What she quippingly calls a 'funny inner feeling', moreover, is almost enough to soothe her apprehensions about time and mortality into simple curiosity. 'What happens in eternity?' Catherine asks, when getting tucked in for bed one night. 'Does one just go on and on?'

'I suppose you just go 'til you're tired,' her mother replies.

The answer is patently unsatisfactory, but upon Catherine's return to Sydney from France her concerns momentarily fade away. Her parents summon the courage to leave Macquarie Street and from the wide balcony of a new house, in Rose Bay, all Catherine's melancholic preoccupations seemed forgotten. She delights in seeing the sun-dappled water through the trees, in being a schoolgirl again, in playing tennis with friends, in going for picnics and car-rides. She barely grieves when her grandfather dies and, when war begins in 1914, she feels it too distant to disrupt her life.

The death of her 'strong and solid' barrister uncle, shot by a sniper at Gallipoli, brings back the tensions bedevilling Catherine. Aged fifteen, she has no truck with the consolation to be found in patriotism and, in *Divided Heart*, she extends her critique of Imperialism to the Church of England — 'a purely national, or rather Imperial, institution bound up with the destiny of the British Empire, and of the British Empire alone.' It is therefore mortal and, unlike a true church, able to drop out of existence. The two years of education in England, at St Felix's, entrench this view.

Catherine writes that her return to Australia marked the start of her real intellectual and spiritual development. But it would be foolish to discard the influences already at work on her. While Catherine dismissed the impressions and opinions she had formed before this time as 'those, first of a child, and then of an adolescent', she admitted too that in the process of writing she realised that childhood and adolescence had taken her past a range of metaphorical landmarks, each important to her ultimate destination.

One that she came to pass in the post-war years was her father. Charles Maclaurin had enlisted in August 1915 and been sent abroad a few months later. He had served in the Australian Auxiliary Hospital, in London, and been discharged in 1917 as a Lieutenant-Colonel. The war, it appears, had eroded the reticence that previously bade him hold his tongue on matters of religion. Catherine recalled him declaring the Catholic Church intolerant and contrasting it, adversely, with paganism. Yet he was also contradictory: his earlier love of Germany and Germans had become a hatred provoked by their wartime destruction of churches. But how could he condemn Germany for shelling churches that he claimed to also despise? Catherine came to regard contradictions like this as those of the head and heart: 'He resembled those poets and writers of the Romantic era who saw in the Church something beautifully picturesque and Old World, though intellectually most of them despised it and socially they thoroughly opposed it.'[27] The tension, as well as a flicker of anxiety, may explain his short-lived decision to turn to God and receive communion in a Presbyterian church; it may also account for why Catherine agreed to her mother's suggestion she take communion.

As Catherine puts it, her mother's suggestion unleashed anew the questioning and introspection that had for so long bedevilled her. It did her no favours:

> I had in fact had no instruction, even of the most elementary kind, in Presbyterian doctrine, but I did know that in nonconformity 'the Sacrament of the Lord's Supper' had the nature only of a commemoration. I knew also that I was not required to make any affirmation of assent to any doctrine, but that I had merely to have my name entered on a card to be registered as a member of the Church. I nevertheless had considerable scruples about publicly proclaiming myself a Presbyterian. I was not sure whether I even believed in God. I was quite sure that I did not believe in the divinity of Christ... Did I believe in the immortality of the soul? I was by no means certain that I did...
>
> I was becoming perturbed at this time about my scepticism, which extended farther and farther upon it, 'til I reached the stage that I thought I could be sure of nothing — not even of my own existence. I had not read Newman at this time, or I might have quoted to myself his famous phrase about the 'all-corroding, all-dissolving scepticism of the intellect in religious enquiries. In the end I consented to receive Communion, largely to please my mother — an unworthy motive, I suppose.[28]

If Catherine gave in as a child, then she also immediately rebelled as a child would. The communion ceremony was underwhelming. In her view, the use of a dinner plate to hold the bread and liqueur glasses to hold what was soon revealed as raspberry syrup rather than wine were undignifying. Yet it was the raspberry syrup, of all things, that most aroused her ire. On leaving, Catherine's mother explained that the congregation were teetotallers all and that unfermented grape juice was too costly to use. But Catherine was aghast and, in what reads as a fit of pique, desisted from further services. The minister turned up at the house to ask why and received both barrels from young Catherine: 'The Church believes that Christ is God, and he used wine, and if you say wine shouldn't be used, you're obviously passing judgement on the Almighty. I always thought it ought to be the other way 'round — God should judge you.'

His protests that the wine was only a symbol had no impact on Catherine: 'Can't you see that it's important that the symbol should be correct? And that, if you use raspberry syrup because you don't approve of wine, you're trying to improve on what Christ did?'

The difference could not be resolved. Catherine's mother sniffed that she was acting like a petulant schoolgirl, but Catherine would not this time back down. 'I never received Communion in the Presbyterian Church again.'[29]

The final disillusionment with the British Empire and the Church of England came next — and brought with it the final erasure of her prejudices against Catholicism and, perhaps more important, the stirring sense that her fears about mortality and eternity might be assuaged by its church. Studying history at the University of Sydney, Catherine came to be ever more critical of the British Empire and Imperialism. George Wood, Challis chair of history, was one influence; another was the work of John Robert Seeley on the way Protestantism had underwritten the bonds of the British Empire. The exception of Ireland would have been conspicuous at any point, but in 1919 it was especially so.

Turmoil over recent events in Ireland — the suspension of the Home Rule Bill in 1914, the Easter Uprising in 1916, the emergence of Sinn Féin in 1918, and the proclamation of an Irish Republic in 1919 — was palpable in Australia, where the existing anti-Catholic and anti-Irish prejudices had been inflamed during the wartime debates over conscription. Anti-Irish sentiment became entangled with anti-Catholic feeling and turned rabid, worse than anything Catherine had seen. Catherine notes some of the more outrageous manifestations: the accusations of 'disloyalty' levelled against Archbishop Daniel Mannix, the scandal over Catholic nun Mary Liguori, the talk of a Jesuit conspiracy to overthrow the monarchy. 'The [Catholic] Church,' Catherine wrote, 'was blamed by such people for everything that happened.'

This atmosphere of outrage and suspicion provoked Catherine. While she was by instinct pro-British and cleaved still to the anti-Catholic views of her class, she could not help but distrust the wild talk and accusations. A lecture on Ireland, given by the rector of St John's College, spurred her to hit the books and change her mind: 'I perceived how much prejudiced and malicious rubbish had been taught me since my infancy and I changed my views on Ireland. I lost the anti-Irish prejudice which is still almost universal among non-Catholics in Australia. This undoubtedly made it easier for me to approach the Church when the time came.'[30]

Her altered views on Ireland led her to reconsider the British Empire. It seemed untenable to perceive it, now, as a 'benevolent institution'. Such a perception could not co-exist with knowledge of its crimes, follies, and misfortunes. Nor could she think that the injustices of its history were perpetual. There had to be some force which rectified them: 'Might not justice ultimately be done, as the great creed of the Church maintained, if not in time, then in eternity?'[31] The creed referred to was the Nicene, whose 'tremendous affirmations' of truth and the eternal struck Catherine with the clarity of a bell.[32] That clarity was important: ongoing debate with her father, as well as her own reading, were making Catherine impatient with the watery intellectual claims in the books her father was pressing on her:

> I suddenly saw that these very clever people and others of their kind, who had written so many volumes stating at enormous length what they had discovered about psychology, about comparative religion, about primitive morals, about the world around them and the heavens above, in the end declared that they knew nothing at all. In fact, they prided themselves on not being able to affirm anything about the ultimate nature of the universe, or even the true nature of the human mind ... They could not even tell their children whether the simplest actions were right or wrong.[33]

The figure who came to bear Catherine's scorn for this was the hapless Presbyterian minister who had tried to convince her that raspberry syrup was just a symbol. John Edwards had delighted in taking up an appointment at St Andrew's Scots Church, Rose Bay in 1913, and he been similarly happy to give Catherine communion. Earnest, thoughtful, and with the characteristic uncertainty of an academic, he was inclined to admit to doubts and second-guessing. An old schoolfriend of Catherine's father, he told Catherine of his struggles with religious belief, including his parting ways with his brother and mother over the question of predestination. Notwithstanding Catherine's refusal to take communion again,

Edwards maintained a connection with her: he volunteered to tutor her in Latin and geometry, ahead of her matriculation, for example.[34] But this did not change Catherine's willingness to be critical. When, in 1921, Edwards gave a speech titled 'Theological Reconstruction', Catherine listened with something close to contempt.

The speech was in large part a call for thoughtful consideration in the cut-and-thrust of theological debate. Suggesting that few, if any theological questions could ever be deemed settled, Edwards argued that reconstruction of Christian theology was ongoing — 'It includes waves and tides advancing and receding, currents and forces clashing or uniting' — and that partakers should be open to different views: 'The Bible can be read so variously!'[35] This reconstruction was also necessary, Edwards argued, as the Presbyterian Church had failed to come to terms with modern developments in science and philosophy. It was becoming irrelevant in a world recovering from the traumas and upheaval of the Great War.

Catherine detected in the speech the figure of Samuel Angus, the theologian whose work was preoccupied with setting aside questions of miracles and divine intervention and immanence in favour of a historically-grounded view of Christianity's emergence and development (as one writer of Angus's views put it, his contrast was between the 'religion of Jesus' and the 'religion about Jesus').[36] Angus had six years before been appointed to a chair of New Testament Exegesis and Historical Theology at St Andrew's College, in Sydney, and in the time since become a quietly provocative figure. The response to Edwards's speech was evidence. The whiff of

Angus's influence led to Edwards being condemned, his beliefs questioned, and his fidelity to the church impugned. An overt backlash to Angus's teachings soon became pronounced.

Catherine, reflecting on the address at a distance of some forty years, called Edwards' address the 'real beginning' of what became known as the Angus case, which ran on for a decade and at certain points threatened to split the Presbyterian church.[37] Averting such a split sapped what little vitality the church had in Australia, in her view, but more damningly crucial was the contrast she increasingly saw with Catholicism. Her father's death, some five years later, removed one of the great sceptics of that religion from her life but left her with salutary words: 'To my mind there is only one truth, and that is objective truth. The so-called inner truth, that sways so many people, especially religious people, and mystics, is not truth at all… But objective truth, if it really is truth, one ought to be able to repeat when you want to and to prove by weighing or measuring or other scientific means.'[38]

These words stay with Catherine as she marries, lives overseas, and then returns to Sydney when it is in the grip of the Depression. Seeing beggars on the streets and abject misery everywhere, Catherine feels newly oppressed and despondent. In the sloughs of that, she recognises that shelving the unresolved problem of religious belief is untenable: it demands a solution. She resolves not to allow her prejudices, or what remains of them, to colour her judgment any longer. Detachment and open mindedness are her bywords. Deciding, and trusting, that some objective truth must be discoverable, Catherine sets aside once and for all any allegiance with Protestant churches: having 'sold the pass' to subjectivists, she believes them dying.

Finally, then, in 1930, Catherine turns to Catholicism. She returns to St Mary's Cathedral and browses a pamphlet on the Catholic Church as champion of human reason. Its argument is sufficiently forceful that she withstands an abrupt parishioner's reprimand and recalls its imprint afterward:

> Here was the starting point of Catholic theology: that the human reason was a valid instrument for the discovery of truth, not only the empirical truth revealed by microscopes and other instruments of research into the sensory world, but of absolute truth transcending this, of those 'ultimates' as Goethe called them, in which we recognise God, the uncreated Creator, the uncaused Cause.[39]

Her journey, at an intellectual and spiritual level, is almost over. Announcing shortly afterward that she intended to be baptised into the Roman Catholic Church, Catherine withstands — or crushes, really — an attempt by Reverend Edwards to dissuade her. 'Soon Presbyterianism will be dead,' she tells him. She attends a midnight mass at St Mary Magdalene's, at Rose Bay, and in the second-hand department of Angus & Robertson's store, on Castlereagh Street, reads a battered copy of Cardinal Newman's *Apologia*. It clinches her conversion, giving her the faith to see that in Catholicism she will find the peace and satisfaction of her restless enquiries and cravings, intellectual and spiritual.

The journey, she thinks, has been pre-ordained from the start. As she finishes, quoting Pascal: 'You would not search for me, if you had not already found me.'[40]

III

Milosz's dictum

Divided Heart's early pages are splashed with vivid colour. Memory provides Catherine with the palette to make bright and striking observations. In the book's latter half, however, that brightness gives way to more muted tones, as though the key signature has changed from C-major to A-minor. Catherine's prose remains sharp, but the material to hand is less amenable to bright rendering. Intellectual preoccupations and disquisitions of course require more measured and thoughtful observations than those which a child can conceivably make; thus the events she describes and the purposes to which she puts them are more gradated, more textured, more adult.

As the tone shifts, so too does Catherine's approach. Where earlier pages took in Catherine's family, the people around her, her schooling, and Sydney geography, later pages feature a narrower set of preoccupations: the book focuses more heavily on her religious questions. But it also begins to move more quickly through time. The years speed up. The pace of new ideas increases. Paradoxically, as this happens, the book begins to feel more insular, more confined. Even as Catherine makes much of the fruits of her university studies and travels overseas, the pleasures and colours of these experiences feel muted. The world beyond the campus fades into static. The turbulence of the 1920s barely registers in *Divided Heart* except in context of Catherine's studies and, later, in the onset of the Great Depression. The enormous capital works and economic boom that attended the decade's first half, the flourishing of modernism, the upheaval of the political world — all are almost entirely absent. Mention of the economic crash and wreckage is fleeting and included only for its relevance to Catherine's religious journey — though it is memorably invoked in descriptions of bootblacks, match-sellers, and impoverished artists chalking pavements with 'gaudy pictures'.

The nature of Catherine's prose remains sufficiently lively that these elisions might justifiably be understood as an author hurrying the reader to the ending. But a question is provoked by Catherine's note of her father's death in 1925. 'I was not able to be with him during the last days,' she writes, 'for I had married the year before and was living with my husband in Schenectady, New York.'

There is no mention of this relationship prior to this; nor does it receive any further mention. The omission is significant. Catherine had excised a vital figure in the intellectual ferment that led to her conversion to Catholicism; in doing so, she also removed any reckoning with the consequences of that conversion — consequences that shaped how she depicted it on the page in *Divided Heart*.

*

Alan Patrick Mackerras came from different stock to his wife. Behind the respectable appearance that his family in the 1900s presented to the world was a more vexed story. Ancestors of his maternal family, the Creaghs, were Irish and Catholic: one had even been Primate of All Ireland. In emigrating to Australia, however, Patrick Creagh also left his family's church. In Sydney he was trained in the law, built a respectable legal practice in the city, and became a Protestant. This blue-eyed man with an imperial beard and aristocratic bearing established a house in Elizabeth Bay, married a fellow Irish emigrant, and had with her four children: two daughters, Lillian and Elizabeth, and two sons, Albert and William. The boys followed their father into legal practice, Lillian remained unmarried for all her days, and Elizabeth, after an unhappy affair, fell in love with the son of one of her father's former clients. James Mackerras was a New Zealander five years younger and possessed of no qualification but a determination to eschew the security of his own father's business for the more uncertain prospect of becoming an orchardist outside Dunedin. He proposed marriage to Elizabeth during a fleeting visit to Sydney in 1897.

Patrick Creagh opposed the marriage but to no avail. By the spring of 1898 Elizabeth was living at Balcutha, New Zealand, heavily pregnant with her first child and watching her husband try valiantly to establish an apple orchard. Already, however, she had felt the circumstances were untenable. She gave birth to a son, Ian, and the following year, unable to bear the cold of the area and the austerity of farm-life, returned to her father's home when she fell pregnant again. Alan was thus born in Elizabeth Bay, a stone's throw from his future wife, in 1899.

But for a short-lived return to Balcutha — ended by the chaos of an avalanche that ruined Mackerras's orchard — Alan and his mother and brother remained in Sydney thereafter. He grew up in much the same locale as Catherine until 1910, when his grandfather moved the family to Glebe Point to save money and pay off a bad debt. While Alan was bereft of a father, he went without the religious strains that Catherine experienced. He and his elder brother attended weekly services at St John's Church of England, in Glebe, and were educated at Sydney Grammar School, in Darlinghurst. Perhaps Alan detected some oddity in the decision to bury his Anglican grandfather in the Catholic section of Waverley cemetery, but this may just as well have been greeted with a shrug, a willingness to defer to the great-aunt and nun who persuaded them to call a Catholic priest. What was less easily shrugged off was the absence of parental love. His father had no contact with him. Though his mother carried to the end of her days a locket with photographs of both boys inside, she was too withdrawn, too broken, too traumatised by the failure of her brief marriage to establish a real or warm connection with them. Both boys instead trained their gazes outward, Alan revealing an inclination for the sciences in his fondness for the telescope and astronomical surveys. His cousin, Nancy Phelan, recalled Alan showing her and her sister the stars in the sky: 'Betelgeuse ... Aldebaran ... Bellatrix... Antares...'[41]

He matriculated in 1918 and the following year began studying mechanical and electrical engineering at the University of Sydney. 'There,' writes Joan Priest, 'he met again the daughter of their old family friends, the Maclaurins' — that is, Catherine.[42]

The Arts course she was studying was a world apart from

his, yet both were unusually serious in their devotion to study and unusually open to discussing that study. On campus but also at parties and dances, they were soon a familiar couple, always engaged in earnest conversation. Priest includes a vivid description of the two, sitting side by side on benches in the cloisters of the university, talking avidly, oblivious to interruption and disruption from the life around them. 'Why they chose the quad, with everyone rushing past, I don't know!' a friend remarked.[43]

Perhaps it was the ability to withstand the noise of everyone else. Nancy Phelan suggested later that Catherine's forthrightness, her precociousness, and brainy willingness to debate opinions and ideas might well have been off-putting or intimidating to young men.[44] Alan, however, seemed not to find it so. A more reserved figure who yearned for warmth and affection, he welcomed Catherine's conversation and interest. An element of play was also at work in the burgeoning relationship. Sharing a summer week with Catherine and some friends at Palm Beach, in 1920, Alan was tagged with a few lines of Thackeray's verse:

> He vexed no quiet neighbour — no
> Useless conquest made
> But by the laws of pleasure — his
> Peaceful realm he swayed.

(Catherine was tagged with an apt line from Shakespeare: 'Farewell the tranquil mind/ Farewell content').[45]

The mutual interest between the two deepened over the subsequent years and the connection established at the university endured. Alan graduated in 1923 and went to work for the Sydney

Municipal Council; Catherine, amid a phase of youthful socialism, immersion in English and Irish history, and increasing debates with her father over religious matters, graduated in 1922 as the runner-up for the University Medal in history. She was by then conscious of sexism, if not entirely willing to agree with all the implications that might follow from that consciousness: her much-admired Professor Wood told Catherine that her final paper in history was every bit as good as a male colleague's, but that he would give that colleague the Medal as it would be 'much more useful for a man.'[46] Catherine's outrage at this remark, as well as her willingness to hold forth, provoked advice from her mother that the best way to exercise her ideals was to concentrate on her studies, marry, have children, and then nurture their talents to make an influence on the broader community.

But despite her graduation Catherine was not ready to move to the next phase of that life quite so quickly. She travelled overseas in 1922, accompanying her father to a celebration of the seven hundredth anniversary of the founding of Padua University, and then to England, where she took tea with Thomas Hardy while her father arranged publication of a book of essays.[47] Catherine's return to Australia came as Alan finished his exams, and in the hinge between adolescence ending and adult life beginning they shared an idyll of a summer. They photographed one another, sailed a skiff, and exchanged light-hearted romantic verse. One of Alan's ran:

> A damsel sweet a face she had
> A youth he wished to take it
> How do I look the damsel said,
> I want to look my best…

Catherine, in turn, offered her own verse, intended as a flourish to photographs of her and Alan sailing: 'Youth at the prow/pleasure at the helm.'

Their engagement followed, and then their wedding, late in April 1924, at St Andrew's Scots Church. John Edwards presided and a reception followed at *Balvaig*, Catherine's parents' home.[48] Barely a fortnight later, the newlyweds were enroute to America, where Alan had organised a position with General Electric.

They had established themselves in Schenectady for barely a year when word of the death of Catherine's father reached them; tragically, Priest notes, that news crossed the Atlantic before Catherine's letter announcing her pregnancy reached Australia.[49] It was followed shortly afterward by Alan's going to the west coast to meet Catherine's newly widowed mother — coming to the US to visit and be present when their child was born — and visit several observatories on the way. He wrote letters to Catherine during that time, detailed missives of the cities he visited and the skies he observed, but peculiarly made no explicit expression of love or affection in those letters. 'There is no greeting of any kind, no endearment, no signature, simply the date,' Joan Priest observed.[50] An explanation is hard to grasp. Was it — as Priest suggests — that Alan felt writing should suffice as an expression of that endearment? Was it that his reserve made him incapable of such an expression?

The point becomes important largely for what it forebodes. If the relationship between Catherine and Alan had hinged, as it first seems, on their exchange of ideas and their willingness to debate all, then the possibility that it might already have begun to cramp or become limited is ominous. As Priest remarks, 'Catherine, warmly articulate herself, away from her own country, with a child expected, would have been looking for and needing such confirmation of his caring.'[51] Yet another reading is that silence, too, might paradoxically be expression of that affection.

Charles was born in November 1925, and eighteen months later he and his parents returned home to Sydney, taking up residence in the hilltop Vaucluse home on Fisher Avenue that Catherine's parents had given them as a wedding present. From there they watched the two ends of the Harbour Bridge arch across the water to their inevitable union, conceived and bore Alastair, in 1928, and resumed a routine of sailing and yachting. Nancy Phelan recalled that both Catherine and Alan were at this time avid and skilful sailors, with an eighteenth-century feeling for literature, and were apt to fling apposite quotes and quips at one another.

Yet if they were happy together then Catherine was feeling the lonely strain of religious tension again. Feeling herself at odds with the Presbyterian church, she attended for a time St Michael's Anglican Church, in Vaucluse, and sent Charles to an Anglican kindergarten school. It goes unmentioned in *Divided Heart*, but in Joan Priest's view this worship was important because it suggested that Protestant churches could not give Catherine what she yearned for: 'She found no inspiration at St Michael's and instead noticed the big flock of people spilling out of the Roman Catholic Church of St Mary Magdalene. There, numbers alone spoke to her.'[52]

It is possible to hear the echo of Catherine's childhood interest in St Mary's Cathedral: again, it is the people going to that church which provokes her curiosity and even her envy. What are they finding there that she cannot find elsewhere?

The onset of the Depression stoked her interest further. Observation of its miseries pushed her to think again about the role of the churches and what they offered to the world — hence the program of reading that swept from Augustine's *Confessions* to Newman's *Apologia*. This brought her, as recounted in *Divided Heart* and here in preceding pages, to the view that reasoning could and should bring her to a decision point. On Christmas Eve, 1931, she attended midnight mass at St Mary Magdalene Church, in Rose Bay. The experience was numinous: 'Surely here was the Spirit.'

The effect of that mass was visible enough for her mother to call Reverend John Edwards, whose attempt to forestall any conversion failed dismally. Edwards's conduct in this debate is depicted in *Divided Heart* in terms almost contemptuous: too gentle to engage in the formidable way that Catherine did, too honest to hold a position in an onslaught of rhetoric, too willing to admit the uncertainties and doubts of religious faith. Catherine's depiction of their conversation is brutal, enough to make the reader wince, yet there is also something unconvincing about it. When Edwards tells Catherine of the necessity of the 'gentle Jesus', she responds with withering force:

> 'Was he so gentle?' I said. 'He used whips to the money changers. He called the Pharisees extortioners and adulterers. He prophesied that blood would flow. He said that he came to cast fire on the earth, remember, to divide families — it's a picture of the Catholic Church. But he was gentle to those who admitted they were sinners. To them he brought not a sword, but peace.'

It is notable that she *says* this, not *asks* — i.e. that she does not admit the possibility that Edwards could be right. It is also notable that the sentences, the examples, the proof of her argument, rush from her in a torrent. Even setting aside the literary element informing this reconstructed conversation, the passage sounds much more akin to platform oratory.

It may well *be* platform oratory. In *Scholars and Gentlemen*, Priest notes the influence on Catherine of Father William Lockington, a Jesuit priest who was, by 1932, coming to the end of a decade's service as headmaster of St Ignatius' College, Riverview. Lockington was a vigorous, practical, and immensely charismatic preacher, blessed with what historian Ursula Bygott called a 'breadth of vision that enabled him to see Australian Catholicism in terms of both its present and future needs.'[53] Lockington was controversial — most notably for his work during the conscription debates of 1917, which had framed him as a principal figure in the 'Jesuit scare' — but his advocacy of the working classes, in the years that followed, had also garnered him some ignominy. He had nonetheless given regular lectures and sermons in public venues up and down the east coast of Australia on topics including patriotism, the Eucharist, and, on the fortieth anniversary of its publication, the papal encyclical *Rerum Novarum*. According to Priest, in 1932 he gave a lecture in Sydney's Town Hall titled *What Catholics Believe*.[54]

Priest posits the lecture as salutary — but it went unmentioned in Catherine's contemporaneous record of her steps toward the Catholic Church and her retracing of those steps thirty years later, in *Divided Heart*. 'Catherine omitted to mention this final step in her journal,' Priest writes, 'perhaps because of the over-simplistic title of the lectures, which would certainly have included an address on the *Apologetics* — the five reasons for belief in God — and a great deal more theological exposition.'[55]

Whatever the explanation, Catherine determined that the Catholic Church was for her. She began instruction at the Sacré Coeur Convent, in Rose Bay, and was then baptised that year by Monsignor O'Reilly, parish priest of St Mary Magdalene's.[56]

All this was then revealed to Alan Mackerras as a *fait accompli*. The books stacked on his wife's bedside had not, apparently, alerted him to the change building in her, but its completion via her baptism could not be ignored. Silence was not an option. Its meaning for them both, and the consequences that would follow, had to be confronted.

*

Conversion of any kind — religious, spiritual, hierarchical, sexual — has its costs. In addition to the emotional and spiritual turmoil that precedes the conversion, and which may make conversion something near to relief, come consequences of all kinds. In the *Confessions*, St Augustine offers an example via the story of Victorinus. A scholar and philosopher in fourth-century Rome who converted to Christianity after a lifetime of pagan worship, Victorinus was apprehensive about his conversion. He was initially afraid that his new religion would offend his powerful friends: 'He thought a storm of enmity would descend upon him.' Faith and joy sheltered him from the bulk of that storm, but he still felt its chill. A law forbidding Christians to teach rhetoric and other literature made it untenable for Victorinus to continue his work as a scholar and he chose accordingly: 'He, having submitted himself to that law, chose rather to forsake those wrangling schools then [sic] thy Word'.[57]

Shakespeare, meanwhile, depicts a cost that is borne by others. In *Henry IV Part 1*, the roustabout Prince Hal is conscious that on becoming king he will have to shake off the influence of the rowdy, zestful Sir John Falstaff, and transform himself into a respectable figure:

> Like bright metal on a sullen ground,
>
> My reformation, glitt'ring o'er my fault,
>
> Shall show more goodly and attract more eyes
>
> Than that which hath no foil to set it off.

At the end of *Part 2*, having become monarch, Hal duly does so in terms that are harsh, public, and absolute. That this comes, for Falstaff, without warning, is one reason it shocks him:

> Reply not to me with a fool-born jest.
>
> Presume not that I am the thing that I was,
>
> For God doth know — so shall the world perceive —
>
> That I have turned away my former self.[58]

Falstaff scrambles to hide his embarrassment with denial — 'I shall be sent for in private to him,' he tells a friend — but accommodating himself to the new gulf that separates them will clearly be difficult; Hal's subsequent command that Falstaff not come again within ten miles of his person makes that distance impossible to bridge. For the audience, Falstaff's shock and new remove is a sadness that lingers; Hal's rejection of his old drinking friend is the most powerful demonstration of his transformation — more powerful than any of the monarchical accoutrements he takes on.

One of the reasons why it is powerful is because it is also honest. Conversion is, ultimately, about honesty: with oneself, at first, but then also with other people about the change that has taken place. What can be tragic about conversion, then — which should, for so many other reasons, be a joyful experience — is when the individual's desire to be authentic to that change in themselves conflicts with their need to belong.

This conflict is especially relevant to Western accounts of sexuality and gender identity. Christopher Isherwood's *A Single Man* builds this quiet tension into everything its ageing English academic protagonist does. George masquerades as a straight man when he is gay; he pretends to grieve the death of a friend when he is grieving the death of his long-term partner. Acknowledging the reality would relieve George of these masquerades, but at social cost. It would also violate the terms of his belonging to Jim. Both kept the relationship secret, just as they did their sexualities. Is George fated to be 'a prisoner of life', as Isherwood mockingly asks, or is it possible for him to find a new accommodation between his authentic self and his need to belong?[59]

Isherwood's answer is ambiguous, but it is impossible to ignore that queer literature has a well-established tradition of tragic endings. Characters come to terms with who they really are, usually find some new belonging with a romantic partner, but at enormous social cost. In Annie Proulx's *Brokeback Mountain*, Ennis del Mar knows from experience that the cost of living openly with Jack Twist will be paid in blood. As he tells Jack: 'There was these two old guys ranched together down home, Earl and Rich — Dad would pass a remark when he seen them. They was a joke, even though they was pretty tough old birds. I was what, nine years old, and they found Earl dead in a irrigation ditch. They'd took a tire iron to him.' In due time, Twist is found dead, apparently victim of an accident. Del Mar knows the reality. 'No, he thought, they got him with the tire iron.'[60]

Both *A Single Man* and *Brokeback Mountain* are from another era, now: social attitudes have so evolved that, today, one's sexual and gender allegiance is much less important to social belonging. In Nigel Featherstone's *My Heart is a Little Wild Thing* (2022), set in 2020, the middle-aged protagonist embraces a homosexual desire that he has for a long time resisted. Moreover, he successfully navigates the process of re-belonging on the terms of that newly awakened sexuality. It is a wholesale contrast to the soldiers-turned-lovers at the heart of Featherstone's *Bodies of Men* (2019), set in World War II, whose decision not to conform makes them vulnerable to arrest from military police.

In all these works, authenticity is imbued with a value higher than that of belonging, even when the cost of the authenticity is dear. That the authenticity achieved is ultimately consoling — if we feel better, for example, that Jack Twist found love, even though he ultimately died because of its revelation — makes it more valuable. It speaks to a Western culture that, since the time Catherine was writing, has come to prize authenticity above almost anything else. It is consistent with an overarching atomisation of society, a privileging of individual identity above any familial or social or institutional belonging.

This makes Catherine's silence on the social consequences of her conversion rather striking. There is nothing of friends shrinking away in disgust, nothing of the scorn that Catherine, by experience, knew Catholics were subject to (nor is there much said about a newfound political affiliation — Catherine did not become a Labor voter overnight). But if there was little cost in her social circles, writings by friends and acquaintances of the Mackerras's make clear that the costs of Catherine's conversion were most exacted in her relationship with her husband. His reaction to the news, writes Joan Priest, 'bordered on shock and despair'. To Alan, Catherine's conversion represented a turning away from all those things they had shared in the past, the common views and complementary outlooks that they had established and argued over on those benches at the University. Catherine must have talked critically about her arguments with her father over his anti-clerical views and rationalism, but Alan had nonetheless believed that their views largely aligned — that they were both 'on the same broad, analytical path'.[61] Discovering that their paths had diverged so markedly was shocking.

Despair, meanwhile, came from knowledge that those paths could not be made to intersect again. Foremost was Alan's outlook, particularly his habitual method of scientific thinking. He could not change this; nor could he abandon his trust in reason and logic, especially for something which carried with it the whiff of grand superstition and a dogmatic insistence that belief could be hammered into fact. His wife, in choosing Catholicism, was striking out in a different direction.

His reaction was compounded by knowledge of his grandfather's own rupture with the Catholic Church. While Catherine came to suspect that Patrick Creagh left the Catholic Church out of snobbery, and others that it was because of his non-Catholic wife, the decision had shaped his descendants and set them an example.[62] Alan, Priest writes, 'wanted nothing to do' with the rescission of that decision. His aversion stemmed less from a sense that conversion would amount to a betrayal of his grandfather and more to a disposition that regarded time as synonymous with progress. Endorsing Catherine's conversion, let alone emulating it himself, would be tantamount to 'being dragged backwards in time.'[63]

A sense of humiliation would be understandable; so too would a time of grim reflection and questioning of what it all meant. It is entirely possible to feel compassion for them both — Alan for the shock and despair of it, for Catherine for struggling alone to a momentous decision, aware that it would be anathema to her husband and feeling driven, therefore, to keep silent about it until silence was no longer possible.

One can question why they both allowed the issue to be the rock on which their relationship foundered. Sixty years from the time Mackerras was writing, it seems needlessly dogmatic. Yet the Australia of today, which treats religion as one element of many in a person's identity, as something private, is not the Australia of Catherine's experience. Nor is the Catholicism of today the Catholicism she deliberately embraced. Catholicism in the 1930s was predominantly shaped by the demographics and concerns of its adherents: families of Irish heritage, drawn overwhelmingly from the working classes, interested in education, almost uniform in the observation of rituals and customs. Contemporary Catholicism in Australia, however, is indelibly shaped by post-World War II migration and the changes ushered in by Vatican II. The result is a pluralistic Catholicism, more affluent, more diverse, more open to participation from lay members, but also one grappling with challenges such as declining attendance at services, a declining number of priests, brothers, and sisters, and questions about its teachings.

In this light, it becomes easier to see why Catherine would see her religiosity as so central to her identity; it is also easier to understand why she and Alan saw it as so central to their marriage.

Neither appears to have entertained any dissolution of it. And yet a distance was imposed between them: not of ten miles, but nonetheless existent. From then on, their paths would have to run in parallel, if only for the sake of their children.

At the urging of Catholic priests, Catherine initially insisted that their three sons be raised in the Catholic Church. Alan resisted. Eventually they compromised, unhappily. Charles, Alastair, and Neil would be educated at Catholic schools before completing their secondary education, as Alan had, at Sydney Grammar School. Any daughters — and Joan and Elizabeth were yet some years off — would follow an equivalent path; any additional sons — Colin and Malcolm were even further off — would follow in the footsteps of their older brothers. The children would make their own decisions about their religion when they were adults.

It is possible to detect an echo of the stricture of Catherine's childhood in this arrangement. Nonetheless, despite the example it suggests, Charles, Alastair, and Neil were educated by the Jesuits at St Aloysius' College; eventually, Colin and Malcolm were too; Elizabeth and Joan were sent to PLC Pymble. Alastair reflected later that his father's compromise was partly borne of the view that children did not learn much before they had learned 'common sense', onset of which he thought coincided with puberty.[64] The Jesuits famously held a different view: 'Give me a child for the first seven years, and I will show you the man,' St Ignatius Loyola said. While this did not altogether hold up for the Mackerras children, as time would reveal, Alan Mackerras also compromised in another way.[65] In another vague echo of the actions of Catherine's father, he refused to allow his children to attend religious classes. He relented when he discovered that passing religious subjects was necessary for them to be eligible to win academic prizes. Perhaps he felt the religious instruction would not matter at such a young age; perhaps he felt some kind of religious instruction was inevitable; perhaps he hoped it might inoculate his children; perhaps he just decided that attaining a prize was more important.

With this agreement made, a new reality was in force. Priest quotes the sad approval it garnered from a teacher at Loreto Convent, Mother Borgia, who became a confidante of Catherine's for years afterward. Borgia called Alan Mackerras a 'true Scot', 'a gallant gentleman', and an honourable man for his determination to untangle the problem, prevent any fracture of the family, and then remain silent about it forever afterward.

Catherine was less inclined. Nancy Phelan argues that Catherine's new faith ruptured the relationship with her husband absolutely: 'It completely negated the things that had drawn them together. She [Catherine] said so later herself. Their strong mutual interest in history now became a battleground — in any discussion she would take one side and Alan the other. Catholicism split them down the middle, in that sense.'[66] Elsewhere, Phelan writes that the split carried into new battlegrounds and was handled in different ways. Music became a difference of opinion and then disdain. To Catherine's eager engagement with debate Alan would demur to argue at all. He could not leap in to disagree when she could become so passionately involved, and so would leave the room entirely rather than contradict her: 'Far more provoking to her temperament,' Phelan observes.[67]

More children made it harder. The love of sailing which had marked the earliest days of their relationship faltered, too. Catherine could go out in a boat less and less, whether because she was minding a young child or, as was periodically the case for at least the next seven years, because she was pregnant. There is an almost literal meaning to Phelan's comment that Catherine and Alan drifted apart.[68]

The duties and obligations of life — earning an income, running a home, raising children — might well have left no time to arrest that drift. Recollections of all the Mackerras children emphasise how noisy and active their home was and how much energy was required to keep everyone in it clothed, fed, and happy amid endless days of school, work, music lessons, dinner parties, holidays, and more. 'Mother worked like a Trojan in those days,' Elizabeth once remarked. 'She used to iron until about midnight … She also had to carry everything — there was just no petrol for shopping.' Alan, who kept in line with social expectations and did not partake in this work, kept more to his study and his job.

Ruptures and divisions are hardly unusual in any relationship, yet this was a division that, while remaining within key bounds, endured throughout, never closing as an old wound might. Rather, like a keloid scar, other divisions and differences built it up. Alastair commented later that his mother encouraged their children to talk much as she did — precociously, with opinion and force. For their father, more minded to quiet and better in one-on-one conversation, this could be alienating: 'He couldn't stand the noise. He used to go off to his study and work.' His passions, too, were not much shared by the children: 'We wouldn't go and look through his telescope … And we didn't like sailing. … Then, at home, we were always playing Wagner, full bore. All these screeching sopranos. He liked Mozart and chamber music.'[69] Joan had similar recollections. At the dinner table, if the children began telling tales and laughing, Alan would get up to leave, saying he had more useful things to do in his study:

> It always happened that it was at the end of the meal, when the talk became serious, and there were really interesting discussions about the young priests and faith and sanctity and such things. And on nights when father went to give lectures at the WEA or to the Sydney Observatory or his Astronomical Association meetings, we were able to say what we liked about religion because he wasn't there to be irritated or annoyed.[70]

A desire to teach and help, so evident to Alan's work colleagues, could find no outlet in the family home.[71] 'With her overwhelmingly forceful personality and equally fine intellect,' writes Priest, Catherine 'simply monopolised the teaching role.' Alan did manage to find some space for doing so, particularly in the bond he built with daughter Elizabeth, but otherwise he effectively vacated the field.

Money was another issue. At a time when social expectations had it that men were providers, Alan's income as an engineer was enough to pay for living expenses for his growing family, but it was hardly of a level with the income and assets enjoyed by Catherine. The home in Vaucluse had been gifted by Catherine's parents, and when they moved to a home in Turramurra, which they dubbed *Harpenden*, she consistently referred to it as 'my house'. Catherine managed her own money and business affairs and made few efforts to hide her financial contributions to their living. As Priest suggests, this was nearly as hard for Alan to bear as her conversion had been.[72]

Then there was the isolation enforced by a lack of physical intimacy. While Alan and Catherine had shared a bed at Vaucluse, they did not at Turramurra; while they continued until 1939 to have children, it appears that sexuality did not become a bond with a purpose beyond procreation. Instead, they became and then remained remote from one another: living with a silence hard to detect amid the din of daily life.

Catherine's satisfaction at having converted did not preclude her from doubts. She spoke often and urgently with Mother Borgia about the rift her conversion had caused, and to Phelan she wondered about leaving her husband: 'I sometimes feel I will have to go.' But she felt bound to him: 'I made a vow and I intend to keep it. He is a good man,' she would add, 'but I simply don't understand him.'[73]

Nor, it seems, did their children — until they became adults. Whether because Alan Mackerras was overshadowed, locked out, or unable to bear the tumult and cacophony of family conversation, each of his children was initially attracted more to Catherine. Charles admitted that as a youth he came close to despising his father; it was only after nine years of separation that he reconsidered his feeling for the man: 'Now suddenly I began to really admire him.'[74] Similar re-evaluations took place with the others, especially once they had left the family home and gatherings were smaller, or even individual. Indeed, in some ways, Alastair suggested, Alan Mackerras was the more influential on them in the long run: 'Most of the seven of us exhibit his generally tolerant and rational attitude to life and to other people.'[75]

But the relationship between Alan and Catherine did not change. Each year their mutual isolation settled on them more and more heavily; indeed, in the way Priest relates it, it became sadly comic. When Charles's wife Judy brought a cooked chicken and hot rolls for lunch one day, Catherine and Alan both exclaimed: 'How nice!' Judy felt gently compelled to say that they could always have it this way — if they wished.

Bound up in that caveat was also an honesty about who Catherine and Alan were and what they each held to. Much as it caused them pain, the division between them was, at very least, an honest one.

*

By the late-1950s, as the children grew up and left home, there came space and time for Catherine to work on projects lengthier and more substantive than articles for the *Bulletin* and book reviews for *Catholic Weekly*. Nancy Phelan, who had established herself as a writer, encouraged her: 'When she [Catherine] said to me, *I think I'll write a book on my family,* I always replied, *Why don't you? Why don't you?*'[76]

In the winter of 1960, Catherine began work on the manuscript that became *Divided Heart*. Ethical dilemmas would have been rife throughout the drafting process: how should she depict the past accurately yet also artfully? How could she be true to what happened, in all its minutiae, after so many years? How much could she trust perception and memory? How, perhaps most pressingly, could she depict people — people who could be mutable, who could be opaque, yet who in a memoir would be pinned down into black and white, transformed into words that would always be inadequate to the immense and complex soul they purported to capture. How could she do it?

Writing about family members, as Catherine intended, would have made this lattermost question especially acute. How to calibrate the depiction of her portrayal of her father, and the vexed relationship with him? How to explore and capture her mother? How to balance the portrayal of her Scottish aunts? How to make them *live* again?

This last question was pertinent: by July 1960, when Catherine began writing, all the people she ended up including were dead. Her father had died in 1925; her aunts had passed away one after the other; her mother had been killed by a blood infection; John Edwards had died in 1942.

There was only one person, by 1960, who had figured in her journey to the Catholic Church and who was still alive. Critically, he was also the person who would be most affected by her putting into writing her conversion. How could she do so, then? How could Catherine depict her relationship with Alan, the man who had provided both intellectual and emotional companionship during her university studies, a period when she was carefully examining her attitudes and prejudices, and with whom she subsequently created a family?

Writers of later generations — not those from what Mackerras would call 'our day of gentler journalism' — would likely not have pondered these questions long.[77] When asked much the same question, as he was frequently, novelist Philip Roth was fond of quoting the Polish writer Czelaw Milosz: 'When a writer is born into a family, the family is finished.'[78] In Roth's view, the artistic work was so paramount in importance that it overrode any notion of familial loyalty, secrecy, or love. Life was material and it was there to be plundered — as Roth did, and as Milosz did, too. 'Writers will insist on *writing* about everything,' Helen Garner has argued. 'We are voracious monsters, ravening beasts who roam the world seeking whom and what we may devour.'[79]

Yet few deny that the wreckage of such feasting may have considerable effect on family members. Nearing the end of his six-volume autobiography, *My Struggle*, Karl Ove Knausgaard admits that his willingness to put so much on the page, and in the public realm, had hurt everyone around him, hurt him, and in a few years' time when his children learned to read would hurt them, too. These self-lacerating words were not overstatement. When he began sending the manuscripts to his family, ahead of publication, one set out in no uncertain terms their opinion: 'Your fucking struggle.' Another replied with different view: 'Verbal rape.'[80] One threatened to sue. Knausgaard's wife, from whom he would divorce, had a nervous breakdown. The process, by the end, was deeply traumatic and the final lines of the whole endeavour are damning. They are perhaps more resonant because they come with an awareness that the toll would continue for some time yet: 'I will never forgive myself for what I have exposed them to, but I did it and I will have to live with it.'[81]

And yet, outside of the books, Knausgaard has expressed a more ambivalent view. On the effect on his family, he agrees that:

> People were hurt, and it was terrible for them when it was happening, but, still, it wasn't the end of the world. There's the guilt for my children, which is constant, which has to do with how I gave our story away to everyone. But, on the other hand, there's a lot of love for them in the book. And when I'm gone that story will also be there for them. I can't, if I'm honest, think that it could be wrong to add a book to the world. How destructive can that be, really?'[82]

Moreover, simultaneous with that temporary pain, comes the duty of literature as Knausgaard sees it — to 'fight fiction', i.e. to push back on the non-existent, the unreal, lies both malevolent and benevolent, and insist on the honesty of fact. The duty is to 'find a way into the world as it is, to open a road we can glimpse for a second or two...'[83]

Confronting what to do about Alan, Catherine chose not to open that road. She omitted him from the work, leaving only the fleeting, ghostly mention of him in the context of her father's death. In doing so, she left out any suggestion that her conversion to Catholicism might involve a cost and she shied away from the result: the satisfaction of her mind and heart, but the loss of something of her heart, too.

Alastair Mackerras, commenting tersely on the omission, writes that his mother chose to avoid intensifying divisions within the family.[84] Priest suggests a subtler reason — that Catherine did not wish to make those divisions public — but also laments a failure of artistic nerve. 'It would have been entirely possible,' she writes, 'to convey their early intellectual accord, the falling in love, and the fact that several years after marriage, when she became a Catholic, Alan was not prepared to change his views.'[85]

If it is difficult to disagree with Priest on this point, it is harder still to disagree with her belief that Catherine carried a strong sense of guilt for the effect of her conversion on her relationship with Alan, and that to assuage that guilt she decided to keep intact the silence that had grown around them both.[86] The manuscript was put away, not to see the light of day: an expression, perhaps learned from Alan, that silence could also be an expression of love.

If it was uncharacteristic of Catherine to choose silence in this way, it was wholly in character that she would be authentic to herself and continue to belong. She would, in short, defy Milosz's dictum. Her family would not be finished.

IV
Perfect wives and perfect mothers

'I was brought up on this legend,' Catherine writes in *Hebrew Melodist*, the biography of musician and composer Isaac Nathan that she published in 1963. For Catherine — as this remark suggests — the project she took up after finishing the manuscript that became *Divided Heart* concerned a deeply familiar subject.

Nathan was Catherine's great-great-grandfather and someone of whom she had heard much while growing up; he was also a figure much relevant thanks to her son Charles's flourishing career in professional music. In this sense, in fact, Catherine's declaration at the beginning of *Hebrew Melodist* — that filial piety is not entirely enough to justify a biography — might be read as both homage to her ancestor but also as expression of affection for her eldest son, to whom the book is dedicated.

Nathan, born in 1790 in Canterbury, England, is an interesting if ultimately minor and frustrating historical figure: minor because of his achievements and the limits imposed on him, and frustrating because there are simply not the sources available to bring him more fully to life. Precociously talented at music, he was employed as a tutor to Princess Charlotte and made a name for himself in the Imperial metropole with *Hebrew Melodies*, an 1814 arrangement that combined supposedly ancient Jewish chants with poems on Jewish subjects that were drafted by Lord Byron — he of 'mad, bad, and dangerous to know' infamy. Nathan's connection with Byron was brief and, in some ways, transactional: the poet had been Nathan's second choice for the job after Sir Walter Scott, and Nathan's choice was, in any event, informed by the length and glimmer of the poet's coattails. But the success of this music was brief. Byron fled England in 1816 and Princess Charlotte died in 1817. Abandoned by his aristocratic benefactors, married, widowed, and married again, Nathan turned from financial necessity to producing a combination of frothy and unmemorable music and tendentious written history. Amid tension over his debts, he ultimately emigrated to Australia, where he acted as a *de facto* music laureate to the New South Wales colony, composing operas and verse for celebrated occasions while tending to an anonymous career as an irascible writer to various magazines and newspapers. He died in 1864, crushed beneath the wheels of a Sydney tram.

It is not hard to see why Catherine would choose to write about Nathan in the wake of her memoir. While she had to travel interstate and overseas for her research, the subject matter was relatively near to hand. Her familial relation also gave her an easy 'in' to her subject, one that she mentions repeatedly, and which allowed Catherine to explore the nexus of family myth and fact. The claim that Nathan was a descendant of the Polish king Stanislaus II, for example, she gave considerable space, even as Catherine admitted that the claim could not be proved.[87] Elsewhere, however, she stressed the connection through inheritance that allowed her to write about Nathan. 'I have in my possession a first edition of *Hebrew Melodist*,' she writes, at one point; at another, she advances the suggestion that Nathan was employed in the royal household as a spy for the Prince Regent, George IV, and declares that this was 'well known to all his descendants'.[88] She adds another claim — that Nathan was sent on a mysterious, secret mission in 1837 by King William IV — but can offer no detail about it whatsoever.

Catherine was also not the first person to have played Boswell to Nathan. He was subject of an extended biographical lecture in 1922, subsequently published, by Charles Bertie; he was also the subject of a full-length biography in 1940 by Olga Somech Phillips. That latter book, however, framed Nathan's significance entirely in terms of his connection with Byron; while Catherine's gives the relationship significant space, her account is by no means defined by it. But her life of Nathan is just as unevenly balanced.

Nathan's career, Catherine admits, peaked with publication of *Hebrew Melodies*, and in having described the attainment of that summit by her book's twenty-second page she leaves a lot of downhill to traverse. Byron exits in the first chapter and in the aftermath Nathan flounders, moving from calamity to disaster at a pace that his biographer struggles to slow. Princess Charlotte dies; Nathan grinds his nose to keep the bailiff away; his first wife dies; his *History of Music* — which even as strong a supporter as Mackerras can only read once, cursorily — is tedious and yet also the next high point of his career. Material that appears interesting, such as suggestion of temper tantrums and of fighting a duel using pistols, is skated over. The twenty-five years that elapse between *Hebrew Melodies* and Nathan's emigration to Australia are covered in almost the same number of pages.

It is when Nathan emigrates, however, that the book most comes to life. Writing of Sydney, circa 1842, Catherine fuses together her own family history, multiple and shifting time signatures, and a perspective that moves sequentially from declaration to imagination to observation to interpretation to description and, finally, to familiarity.

> The Botanical Gardens were an almost treeless waste where even yet "blacks" might occasionally perform half-hearted and dispirited corroborees. Lady Maclaurin, Isaac Nathan's granddaughter, who was born in Sydney three years after his arrival, could recall watching such a corroboree from the windows of her home in Macquarie Street, which was the street of finest residences within the city proper. Hyde Park was almost barren ground in 1842; across it one could see the old St Mary's Cathedral, and the dignified though still unfinished building of Sydney College. The terraces were creeping around Woolloomooloo Bay; on South Head Road the cattle wandered, stumbling along the ruts. But Sydney in 1842 was already lit by gas; in John Rae's drawings we can see, on every corner, those picturesque street lamps, now finishing their long career of usefulness as electric lights in many a suburban garden. There were splendid carriages prancing in the streets; there were steam-boats, long-funnelled and paddle-wheeled, cruising on the still-unpolluted waters of the harbour; and already in the daily

press, vigorously if somewhat scandalously written, a campaign had begun for the building of a railway to Parramatta.[89]

This is where *Hebrew Melodist* offers its best passages. The apprehension of Sydney's growth and development is keen; the insight to the way that class and power functioned in the city is admirable; the willingness to expand the scope beyond Nathan (who remains more viewed than understood) gives latter chapters of the book a bustling cosmopolitanism reminiscent of Alythea Hayter's *A Sultry Month*.[90] Personalities vivid and colourful — Charles Windeyer, George Gipps, Ludwig Leichhardt, among others — cross the page and provide landmarks to apprehend Nathan's efforts at ingratiation and artistic satisfaction. Meanwhile, the family history continues through Catherine's tracing of the life of Charles, Nathan's eldest son, who became a famed surgeon and anaesthetist on Macquarie Street.

As a biographer, Catherine's interest in her subject is evident and so too is her appreciation of his milieu. Yet she is also characteristically willing to step into the narrative and set the reader straight. She all but rolls her eyes at suggestions of other writers, for example: 'Why, I cannot imagine…' she writes of one spurious claim.[91] 'I think that it deserves some consideration,' she writes, correcting another biographer.[92] She speculates, and then decides, on the page, her interpretation: 'I think it almost certain….'[93] At times, she foregrounds an empathetic imagining: 'I think that these additional words must have been prompted by the misery in Nathan's expressive face; and am I almost prepared to wager that, as he pressed Byron's hand and pocketed his £50, there were tears in those dark Hebrew eyes…'[94] She includes the biographer's efforts to overcome gaps in the record: 'I can find no record of any correspondence between them...'[95]

Tart, crisp, and brooking no argument, Catherine exercises her critical judgement widely. The novels of Nathan's first wife are 'no more unreadable today than are most of the minor effusions of Regency England'. Of the man himself, Catherine is at times positively cutting. The *Hebrew Melodies* that supply her title and made Nathan's name is in her view a slight thing, 'too completely of its age and date ever to become a classic'; his prose works, meanwhile are 'extraordinarily verbose'.[96] To read half a dozen pages of Nathan's *History of Music*, a famous work on singing and music, 'requires heroic effort on the part of the modern reader,' Catherine tells us.[97] Winningly, her desire to perpetuate Nathan's memory does not lead her to over-exaggerate or whitewash her subject.

And yet the book is not distant from the reader. There is a palpable warmth in Catherine's willingness to invite the reader with her. She repeatedly refers to 'us' and extends invitations for what 'we' might understand about Nathan at a century's remove. She is anxious, too, to show why readers should be interested in Nathan and his place in Australian cultural life: 'We have all learnt *The Destruction of Sennacherib* at school,' she says, casually, at one point.[98]

To consider *Hebrew Melodist* as a mirror of Catherine's interests and blinkers is fruitful. She is, unsurprisingly, attentive to religious affiliation. Nathan's father, Menehem Mona, was a Jewish scholar and almost certainly Cantor of Canterbury Synagogue who intended for Isaac Nathan, as the eldest son, to be a rabbi. The discovery that Nathan enjoyed music more than Hebrew was followed by his slow distancing from Judaism. Nathan was married in an Anglican church and in a synagogue, but his wife was a reluctant convert and their children were baptised into the Church of England: notably, Charles became a fervent Christian, even a warden and trustee of St James's, King Street.[99] Catherine is sharp and pragmatic about the factors at play in all these decisions, arguing that social reasons were paramount.[100] In Australia, though, Nathan appears to have crossed religious lines, or even deliberately cultivated some ambiguity about them. He was conductor of the choir at St Mary's Cathedral, and he was buried in the Camperdown Cemetery that William Broughton — an Anglican bishop — had consecrated in 1849.[101] There is no evidence that he was baptised, but it is impossible not to consider it a live possibility.

Another conspicuous point is the attention she draws to Nathan's efforts to adapt Indigenous Australian music and chants. Catherine was not entirely enamoured with the results, both for ethical reasons but also for the artistic failure of taking the 'wild originals' and taming them into 'stilted Victorian verse and conventional Victorian harmonies'.[102] It would have been better, she relates, if he had transcribed those chants as they were rather than altering them so. What is notable is the ability to communicate praise and critique in the same breath: appreciation for the effort of taking the culture and art of Indigenous Australians seriously, but reproach for failing to take that effort further, and appreciate it for what it is, rather than what it could be.

Last is Catherine's clear preoccupation with what art means in Australia. In *Scholars and Gentlemen*, Joan Priest relates repeated instances of Catherine expressing dissatisfaction with Australian artistic and cultural life. Such dissatisfaction spurred her to push her children to Europe for their education and training. 'She used to say,' Joan recalled, 'that the essence of Australian beauty was not the same as the essence of the beauty to be found in Europe — just no comparison between the two. Everything European was, *ipso facto*, marvellous.'[103]

That Catherine was echoing common views is clear enough. This was the era when Australians of any artistic ambition left the place — see John Russell, Alan Moorehead, Sidney Nolan, Edith Fry, Patrick White. It was the era when the world's artistic centres were always far away and always the only point of reference. It was before A. A. Phillips identified the influence of the 'cultural cringe', and before Robin Boyd argued that white Australians, as foreigners to the continent, were unable to commit to the real ideas that would make for great art.[104]

And yet, by the 1940s and 1950s, the argument that Australia could have no great art, that it could not be compared favourably with art produced in Europe, was losing its currency. The argument that European terms should be the basis of aesthetic judgements was also coming into question. An emerging, distinctive national identity, with its own artistic life and culture, was becoming palpable. White, who returned to Australia in 1947, suggested something of the difference between art in Europe and art in Australia by saying that, in the first, writing was the 'practice of an art by a polished mind in civilised surroundings'; in Australia, it was creating 'completely fresh forms out of the rocks and sticks of words'.[105]

Catherine was never sympathetic to this nascent Australian art, but Alan Mackerras was. As his children travelled and tasted that European beauty, he urged them to rethink the terms on which they were doing so. During a walking holiday in Switzerland, he argued with Joan and Elizabeth about art in Australia and in Europe. As Priest writes: 'He admitted frankly to the girls that he felt that their mother had been too strong an influence on them in regard to everything European being better than everything Australian...'

In *Hebrew Melodist*, it is possible to sense Catherine trying to build up an artistic landscape in Australia which *might* be a valid, if still inferior, corollary to that European landscape. Notwithstanding her view that his life in Australia was generally unhappy and unfruitful — later the subject of some rebuttal — Catherine argues that Nathan was the 'father of Australian music' who laid the musical foundations on which others built, thereby aiding the exploration of the country of the mind.[106] Nathan's efforts to bring European music to Australia, and his efforts to graft it into the culture emerging in Sydney and to combine it with that of Australia's Indigenous peoples, were vital and, for her, deserving of remembrance.

Just as it is possible to see *Hebrew Melodist* as an expression of affection for her great-grandfather *and* for her son, Charles, it is also possible to see it as Catherine's reaching for a unity of her own: between the European culture and art that she loved and the country in which she had also made a home.

*

Hebrew Melodist was published early in 1963. It was reviewed widely and garnered respectful if not uncritical notices.[107] For a debut full-length work it is undoubtedly promising, and Catherine does not appear to have been discouraged by the response. She soon set about on a new project, one that would continue her exploration of her family by charting the life of her grandfather, Normand Maclaurin. This would be a much greater endeavour, since the extant material on Maclaurin was more abundant and more diverse, and his life more far-ranging in its activities.

Work on that project was ongoing in the subsequent decade, as were discursions into shorter works. Catherine condensed her *Hebrew Melodist* research for Isaac Nathan's entry in the *Australian Dictionary of Biography* (*ADB*) and researched and wrote an entry for his son Charles Maclaurin (her great-grandfather). Expanding that research, she celebrated the surgery in which he pioneered anaesthetics, again drawing on her memory and interaction:

> There was the horsehair and mahogany examination couch which was too high to climb unaided; and a tall pair of antiquated scales, all black and white, most beautifully made, on which I longed to stand, but was forbidden. I did not dare to open the glass front of the great, massive bookcase, through which there shone the gilded titles of well-known surgical handbooks from a day long past.[108]

Entries for the *ADB* on musicians William Wallace and Stephen Marsh (both contemporaries of Nathan's) also followed from her pen, as did a stream of reviews, essays, and letters for periodicals including *Catholic Weekly*, the *Bulletin*, *Canon*, and more.

It is impossible not to see all this output and these plans and regard it with some tinge of sorrow: not for its quality but for its coming so late in her life. 'I always wanted to write,' Catherine told Hazel de Berg, in 1974.[109] What got in the way, for so long, of doing that? Deborah Levy — a woman and writer some two generations younger than Catherine — guessed once that no woman could be ruthless enough to pursue her dreams to the expense of everyone else. 'We felt guilty every time we absented ourselves from the wishes and desires of those who depend on us for their well-being and for cashflow.'[110]

There is nothing to suggest that Catherine did not make space for her literary interests and passions, nor that she ever expressed disquiet for not writing more during the years her children were growing up. And yet one thinks of Alan's consistent withdrawal to his study. One thinks of the time he spent sailing his yacht on Sydney harbour while Catherine was pregnant and minding children. One thinks of his visiting friends, calling in on the way home, of his building model yachts in quiet solitude, while Catherine mothered, cooked, cleaned, did the ironing at midnight, and *still* mustered the energy to be so vivid and influential a figure in the lives of her children.[111]

One thinks, too, about the sacrifices she made with the manuscript that became *Divided Heart*: compromised in its content by consideration for her husband, and then for thirty years — until both were dead — held back from publication for reasons that were almost certainly the same.[112] One thinks of the loneliness that prompted Catherine's complaint to Nancy Phelan, after publication of *Hebrew Melodist*, that Alan was not interested and did not read the book. That the specific claim might be untrue, as Joan Priest suggests, does not erase the underlying grievance of it.[113] Then one thinks of the research that went into the Normand Maclaurin biography — so far advanced, but ultimately never finished and never published.[114]

And then one thinks of a poem Catherine wrote and published in 1922, when that connection with Alan was still untroubled by religion and not yet busied with children and work:

Love spoke to me and asked me to forego
    My whole life-work and all my wonted joys.
        Love cried aloud with mighty trumpet-voice,
'See, I alone am real in all the show
Of vain and worldly things.' I said, 'Ah, no!
    You sport with men, as though they were your toys,
        Roughly disturb their life's long even poise,
And make them sad; you shall not use me so.'

Expressed, here, was a determination to remain poised and to do what she wanted, not to submit to the distorting force of love and its attendant burdens. And yet, as that poem goes on to illuminate, there are snares and tricks — social strictures and pressures, creeping expectations that accrete over time — that erode that determination:

Love whispered mockingly: 'I have not met
    The man that could resist me many days.'
I frowned and turned away in foolish pet,
    But he pursued me with his skilful ways.

And while I cried: 'You have not caught *me* yet,'

He slipped into my heart; and there he stays!'[115]

Writing of her relationship with her parents and her awareness, even as a child, that she came a distinct second in their affections, Catherine commented that 'few in my experience are the women who are perfect wives and perfect mothers, too.'[116] The comment was another that could not have come from such a young person. Yet it also could only have come from someone with enough awareness and compassion to recognise the faults in herself — faults that she shared with others. If she was not the perfect wife to Alan, then neither was he the perfect husband to her: at the end, they were companions enough to raise seven brilliant children and, despite division, to hold true to their beliefs and their vows.

*

Alan died in 1973, following a prolonged illness caused by a stroke. To the end, notwithstanding their distance, Catherine prayed for him; to the end, she kept her silence and made no move to publish her memoirs.[117]

Despite the costs to her relationship, and indeed her increasingly sceptical regard for the changes to Catholic liturgies that followed Vatican II, she never came to regret her decision to become a Catholic.[118] The declaration that she wrote in her journal shortly after her baptism held true for forty-five years, until her death in 1977: 'In the Catholic Church I had found that which satisfies the restless enquiries of the mind and the persistent cravings of the heart.'[119]

Acknowledgements

This essay was first suggested late in 2018. Throughout the years that have elapsed, Damien Freeman, principal policy advisor to the PM Glynn Institute, at the Australian Catholic University until 2023, and now a research fellow at Catholic Schools NSW's Kathleen Burrow Research Institute, has been especially patient in awaiting receipt of it. For the considerable delays and much too frequent radio silences that have interrupted transmissions between Canberra and Sydney, I have made many apologies but never enough expressions of gratitude for the provocation that the assignment afforded. Reading and writing about Catherine Mackerras's life has been stimulating. I am grateful for the opportunity Damien afforded for me to do this work, and acknowledge and thank him for his patience, his generosity, and his encouragement.

Michael Casey, director of the PM Glynn Institute, at the Australian Catholic University, has been similarly encouraging and patient, particularly after the formal research fellowship that underpinned this work came and went without a finished essay. I am grateful to Michael for his support, encouragement, and understanding.

Notes

1 'Cultural diversity', '1301.0 – Year Book Australia, 2008', *Australian Bureau of Statistics*, 7 February 2008, <https://www.abs.gov.au/ausstats/abs@.nsf/7d12b0f6763c78caca257061001cc588/636F496B2B-943F12CA2573D200109DA9?opendocument>, accessed 9 May 2024; 'Religious affiliation in Australia: Exploration of the changes in reported religion in the 2021 census', *Australian Bureau of Statistics*, 4 July 2022, <https://www.abs.gov.au/articles/religious-affiliation-australia>, accessed 9 May 2024.

2 Catherine Mackerras, 'An autobiographical fragment', *Twentieth Century*, Winter 1963, pp. 322–26.

3 Catherine Mackerras, 1991, *Divided heart: The memoirs of Catherine B. Mackerras*, Little Hills Press, Crows Nest, p. 19.

4 Op. cit., p. 24.

5 Op. cit., pp. 23–25.

6 Not, as Catherine keenly reminded readers, the 'modern' version built in the 1930s, which she disdained on grounds that it 'reflects a softening of the brain and character, as well as a softening of the heart'.

7 Op. cit., p. 37.

8 Op. cit., p. 51.

9 Op. cit., p. 36–37. Catherine's regard for the Empire does appear, the above notwithstanding, to have been mutable. She relates that seeing the British naval flag floating in the north-east winds each morning was her substitute for morning prayers: see pp. 38–39.

10 Op. cit., p. 54.

11 Op. cit., p. 60.

12 Ibid.

13   Op. cit., p. 61.
14   Op cit., pp. 124–25.
15   Deborah Levy, 2021, *Real Estate*, Hamish Hamilton, London, p. 227–28.
16   Op cit., pp. 14–15.
17   Mackerras, 1991, p. 18.
18   Op. cit., p. 125.
19   Patrick Riley, 2004, *Character and conversion in autobiography: Augustine, Montaigne, Descartes, Rousseau, and Sartre*, University of Virginia Press, Virginia, p. 1.
20   Philippe Lejeune and Claude Leroy (eds), 1995, *Le tournant d'une vie*, Cantre de Recherches Interdisciplinaires sur les Textes Modernes de l'Université de Paris X, Paris, p. 7.
21   Mackerras, 1991, p. 70.
22   Op. cit., p. 71.
23   Mackerras's mother suggests that it was Sally's 'stern Presbyterian upbringing' that endured and stopped her going.
24   Op. cit., p. 34.
25   Op. cit., p. 105.
26   Op. cit., p. 106.
27   Op. cit., p. 129.
28   Op. cit., pp. 139–41.
29   Op. cit., p. 142.
30   Op. cit., p. 151.
31   Op. cit., p. 156.
32   Op. cit., p. 135.
33   Op. cit., p. 161.
34   Ian Edwards, 1998, *The faith of a heretic: The life and works of the Rev John Edwards and some thoughts on the Presbyterian Church in Australia*, Fast Books, Sydney, pp. 17–18.
35   John Edwards, 1921, *Theological reconstruction: A plea for freedom*, Angus & Robertson, Sydney, pp. 8–9.

36 Alan Dougan, 1979, 'Angus, Samuel (1881–1943)', *Australian Dictionary of Biography*, vol. 7. See also: Alan Dougan, 1971, *A backward glance at the Angus affair*, Wentworth Books, Sydney.

37 Mackerras, 1991, p. 165; for background to the Angus case, see Susan Emilsen, 1991, *A whiff of heresy: Samuel Angus and the Presbyterian Church in New South Wales*, New South Wales University Press, Kensington, pp. 164–272.

38 Mackerras, 1991, p. 172.

39 Op. cit., p. 179.

40 Op. cit., p. 192.

41 Nancy Phelan, 1990, *A kingdom by the sea*, Imprint, Sydney, p. 116.

42 Joan Priest, 1986, *Scholars and gentlemen: A biography of the Mackerras family*, Boolarong Publications, Spring Hill, p. 28.

43 Hutchinson, in Priest, 1986, p. 28.

44 Nancy Phelan, 1987, *Charles Mackerras: A musician's musician*, Oxford University Press, Melbourne, pp. 25–26.

45 Priest, 1986, p. 32.

46 Op. cit., p. 24. In an interview with de Berg in 1974, Catherine identifies that colleague as Victor Windeyer, justice of the High Court (1958–72).

47 Charles Maclaurin, 1923, *Post mortem: Essays, historical and medical*, Jonathan Cape, London.

48 'Weddings — Mackerras–Maclaurin', *Daily Telegraph*, 24 April 1894, p. 3.

49 Priest, 1986, p. 42.

50 Op. cit., p. 43.

51 Ibid.

52 Op. cit., p. 46.

53 Ursula M.L. Bygott, 1980, *With pen and paper: The Jesuits in Australia, 1865–1939*, Melbourne University Press, Carlton, p. 107.

54 I have been able to find no coverage of this lecture.

55 Priest, 1986, p. 50.

56 Alastair Mackerras, in Mackerras, 1991, p. 5.

57 St Augustine, 1638, *The confessions of S. Augustine, bishop of Hippon and D. of the church*, trans. S.T.M., Paris, p. 273. John Chadwick's translation refers, perhaps more illuminatingly, to 'schools of loquacious chattering'.

58 Shakespeare, *Henry IV, Part 2*, Act 5, scene 5, 55–58.

59 Christopher Isherwood, 2010, *A Single Man*, Vintage, London, p. 6.

60 Annie Proulx, 'Brokeback Mountain', *New Yorker*, 13 October 1997, pp. 74–85.

61 Priest, 1986, p. 50.

62 Phelan, 1987, p. 30.

63 Priest, 1986, pp. 50–51.

64 Alastair Mackerras, in Mackerras, 1991, p. 6.

65 According to Priest, Charles appreciated deeply the familiarity with Catholic art that his religious education had given him but felt never compelled to become a Catholic. Alastair felt the compulsion quietly and quietly acted upon it, choosing to be baptised in deference to his father only once he was living out of home. Neil was baptised, as was Joan, who had once disdained the tension she had felt in her father's refusal to allow her to take communion. Elizabeth chose not to become a Catholic, nor eventually did Malcolm, but Colin did and in some ways his struggles with religion echo his mother's. Saying later that the process of moving away from belief was 'slow and traumatic', Colin had decided well before he was eighteen to be baptised. This coincided with the destabilising experience of university, where questions and debate about Catholic theology left him doubtful and unhappy; study and life overseas gave him the distance to think that Catholic doctrine, particularly around sex, was psychologically harmful. He subsequently abandoned it.

66 Phelan, in Priest, 1986, p. 51.

67 Phelan, 1987, p. 35.

68 Op. cit., p. 34.

69 Priest, 1986, pp. 53–54.

70 Op. cit., p. 78.

71 The inability to find such a role may have prompted Alan's interest in the Wilsons, neighbours in Turramurra; John Wilson recalled Alan Mackerras's visits to their home and his kindly interest and conversation with him while a child. See Priest, 1986, p. 66.

72 Op. cit., p. 63.

73 Op. cit., p. 80.

74 Op. cit., pp. 98,

75 Alastair Mackerras, in Mackerras, 1991, p. 5.

76 Priest, 1986, p. 304.

77 Catherine Mackerras, 1963, *The Hebrew melodist*, Currawong Publishing Co., Sydney, p. 31.

78 Blake Bailey, 2021, *Philip Roth: The biography*, W.W. Norton, New York, p. 316.

79 Helen Garner, 2017, *True stories: Collected non-fiction*, Text, Melbourne, p. 304.

80 Karl Ove Knausgaard, 2018, 'How Karl Ove Knausgaard's relatives felt about Karl Ove Knausgaard's book', *Slate*, 19 September, <https://slate.com/culture/2018/09/my-struggle-book-6-excerpt-the-knausgaard-family-reaction.html>, accessed 1 May 2023.

81 Karl Ove Knausgaard, 2018, *The end*, trans. Don Bartlett, Harvill Secker, London, p. 1153.

82 Joshua Rothman, 2018, 'Karl Ove Knausgaard looks back on "My Struggle"', *New Yorker*, 11 November, <https://www.newyorker.com/culture/the-new-yorker-interview/karl-ove-knausgaard-the-duty-of-literature-is-to-fight-fiction>, accessed 1 May 2023.

83 Ibid.

84 Alastair Mackerras, in Mackerras, 1991, p. 4.

85 Priest, 1986, p. 310.

86 Speaking with Hazel de Berg in 1974, Catherine declared her husband was 'extremely tolerant and understanding [about her conversion], for which I was always very grateful to him.'

87 Mackerras, 1963, p. 11.
88 Mackerras, 1963, pp. 20, 36.
89 Op. cit., p. 62.
90 Alythea Hayter, 1992, *A sultry month: Scenes of London literary life in 1846*, Quartet, London.
91 Op. cit., p. 18
92 Op. cit., p. 52.
93 Op. cit., p. 51
94 Op. cit., p. 25.
95 Op. cit., p. 26.
96 Op. cit., p. 23.
97 Op. cit., p. 42.
98 Op. cit., p. 19. That students in the twenty-first century do not, I am sure, would a disappointment to Catherine.
99 Op. cit., p. 119.
100 Op. cit., p. 39.
101 Olga Phillips adds that he was 'alienated from Judaism'; Catherine, for her part, subtly calls this into question with her point that Phillips was in error to claim that Nathan's gravestone was inscribed in Hebrew: 'The inscription is in English!': see Mackerras, 1963, p. 119.
102 Op. cit., p. 102.
103 Priest, 1986, p. 208.
104 A. A. Phillips, 1950, 'The cultural cringe', *Meanjin*, vol. 9, iss. 4, pp. 299–302; Robin Boyd, 2012, *The Australian Ugliness*, Text, Melbourne, p. 162.
105 Patrick White, 1958, 'The prodigal son', *Australian Letters*, vol. 1, iss. 3.
106 For a rebuttal of Mackerras's characterisation of Nathan, see Graham Pont, 1993, 'The rediscovery of Isaac Nathan; or "Merry freaks in troub'lous times"', *Australian Jewish Historical Society Journal*, vol. 12, no. 1, November, pp. 42–53.
107 Martin Long's is representative: see Martin Long, 'Migrant Melodist', *Bulletin*, 30 March 1963, pp. 38–39.

108 Priest, 1986, p. 302.

109 Catherine Mackerras interviewed by Hazel de Berg, 9 January 1974, NLA Oral History, TRC 1/751, p. 1:2.

110 Levy, 2021, p. 78.

111 Deborah Levy, again, is provocative: 'To strip the wallpaper off the fairy tale of the Family House in which the comfort and happiness of men and children have been the priority is to find behind it an unthanked, unloved, neglected, exhausted woman.' See Levy, 2018, *Cost of living*, Hamish Hamilton, London, p. 23.

112 In doing so, Catherine eschewed the example of Helen Garner, who noted that writing was a 'risky business': 'Every time I write a book, I lose a husband.' See Garner, 2017, p. 306.

113 Priest writes that Alan Mackerras was in fact very proud of Catherine's writing and recounts that he struck up a conversation about the book with some extended family members. His failure to express this, though, was 'part of the complexity of his feeling towards her'.

114 A typescript remains among the Mackerras papers at the State Library of NSW.

115 Mackerras, 'Sonnet', in J. Le Gay Brereton (int.), 1922, *Australian university verse: An undergraduate anthology*, Universities of Australia, Sydney, p. 40.

116 Mackerras, 1991, p. 65.

117 Catherine told Hazel de Berg in 1974 that she intended to write her memoirs: see Catherine Mackerras interviewed by Hazel de Berg, 9 January 1974, NLA Oral History, TRC 1/751, p. 8.

118 Alastair Mackerras in Mackerras, 1991, pp. 8–9; Edmund Campion, 1997, *Great Australian Catholics*, Aurora Books, Richmond, pp. 80–83.

119 Quoted in Priest, 1986, p. 52.

THE KAPUNDA PRESS
an imprint of Connor Court Publishing
in association with the PM Glynn Institute

GENERAL EDITOR
Damien Freeman
Honorary Fellow, Australian Catholic University
Research Fellow, Kathleen Burrow Research Institute, Catholic Schools NSW
Fellow, Robert Menzies Institute, University of Melbourne

2021
SHADOW OF THE CROSS
CATHOLIC SOCIAL TEACHING AND AUSTRALIAN POLITICS
Greg Craven
Tony Abbott – Philip Booth – Sandie Cornish – Kevin Rudd
Frank Brennan

BURAADJA
THE LIBERAL CASE FOR NATIONAL RECONCILIATION
Andrew Bragg

2020
FAITH'S PLACE
DEMOCRACY IN A RELIGIOUS WORLD
Bryan S. Turner – Damien Freeman
Dean Smith – Luke Gosling – Ursula Stephens – Jocelyne Cesari
Jim Franklin – Robert Hefner – Riaz Hassan – David Saperstein
M. A. Casey

THE NEW SOCIAL CONTRACT
RENEWING THE LIBERAL VISION FOR AUSTRALIA
Tim Wilson

TRIBALISM'S TROUBLES
RESPONDING TO ROWAN WILLIAMS
Damien Freeman

Rowan Williams – Ethan Westwood – M. A. Casey
Cristina Gomez – Nigel Zimmermann – Annette Pierdziwol
Kerry Pinkstone – Amanda Stoker – Scott Stephens
Ben Etherington – Anthony Ekpo – Austin Wyatt – Sandra Jones

2019
STORY OF OUR COUNTRY
LABOR'S VISION FOR AUSTRALIA
Adrian Pabst

THE MARKET'S MORALS
RESPONDING TO JESSE NORMAN
Damien Freeman

Jesse Norman – Marc Stears – Greg Melleuish – Adrian Pabst
Amanda Walsh – Parnell McGuinness – Michael Easson
David Corbett – Tom Switzer – Cris Abbu – Tanya Aspland
Leanne Smith – M. A. Casey

NONSENSE ON STILTS
Rescuing Human Rights in Australia
Damien Freeman – Catherine Renshaw
M. A. Casey – Nicholas Aroney – Emma Dawson
Terri Butler – Jennifer Cook – Bryan Turner – Tim Wilson

FEDERATION'S MAN OF LETTERS
PATRICK MCMAHON GLYNN
Anne Henderson
Anne Twomey – Suzanne Rutland – Patrick Mullins – John Fahey
Peter Boyce

2018
TODAY'S TYRANTS
Responding to Dyson Heydon
Damien Freeman
J. D. Heydon – Frank Brennan – Anne Henderson – Paul Kelly
M. A. Casey – Peter Kurti – M. J. Crennan – Hayden Ramsay
Shireen Morris – Michael Ondaatje – Sandra Lynch
Catherine Renshaw

CHALICE OF LIBERTY
Protecting Religious Liberty in Australia
Frank Brennan – M. A. Casey – Greg Craven

www.ingramcontent.com/pod-product-compliance
Lightning Source LLC
Chambersburg PA
CBHW050555160426
43199CB00015B/2666